Inspiration Is Key

Inspiration Is Key

Unconventional Strategies to Motivate and Support Students

Victor Sgambato

ROWMAN & LITTLEFIELD
Lanham • Boulder • New York • London

Published by Rowman & Littlefield
A wholly owned subsidiary of The Rowman & Littlefield Publishing Group, Inc.
4501 Forbes Boulevard, Suite 200, Lanham, Maryland 20706
www.rowman.com

Unit A, Whitacre Mews, 26-34 Stannary Street, London SE11 4AB

Copyright © 2016 by Victor Sgambato

All rights reserved. No part of this book may be reproduced in any form or by any electronic or mechanical means, including information storage and retrieval systems, without written permission from the publisher, except by a reviewer who may quote passages in a review.

British Library Cataloguing in Publication Information Available

Library of Congress Cataloging-in-Publication Data
Names: Sgambato, Victor, author.
Title: Inspiration is key : unconventional strategies to motivate and support students / Victor Sgambato.
Description: Lanham : Rowman & Littlefield, [2016]
Identifiers: LCCN 2015041472 (print) | LCCN 2015047914 (ebook) | ISBN 9781475824988 (hardcover : alk. paper) | ISBN 9781475824995 (pbk. : alk. paper) | ISBN 9781475825008 (electronic)
Subjects: LCSH: Motivation in education.
Classification: LCC LB1065 .S49 2016 (print) | LCC LB1065 (ebook) | DDC 370.15/4—dc23
LC record available at http://lccn.loc.gov/2015041472

∞™ The paper used in this publication meets the minimum requirements of American National Standard for Information Sciences—Permanence of Paper for Printed Library Materials, ANSI/NISO Z39.48-1992.

Printed in the United States of America

Contents

Foreword: Keys to Successful and Rewarding
    Teaching   *Walt Wheeler*   vii

Preface   ix

Acknowledgments   xi

Introduction   1

PART I: *YOU* RETAIN THE POTENTIAL TO INSPIRE, MOTIVATE, AND SUPPORT YOUR STUDENTS

1 Joys of Teaching   7

2 Fellowship: The Feel of Support   15

PART II: PROFESSIONAL ADVICE FOR DEALING WITH YOUR STUDENTS

3 Learning from Classroom Experience   19

PART III: TOOLS THAT SUCCEED: UNCONVENTIONAL APPROACHES AND STRATEGIES

4 Unique and Unorthodox Approaches in Education   41

5 Are You Listening to Your Students?   49

6 Cooperative Classroom Environment   53

7 The Seat of Distinction: Promoting *Sensitivity*, *Trust*, and *Comfort*   71

PART IV: IS THERE MORE THAT CAN WE DO?

8 Support Groups for Adolescents   81

9 Multicultural Education   95

Notes   99

Appendix   101

About the Author   123

Foreword

Keys to Successful and Rewarding Teaching

Reading this book will change how you look at the art of teaching. I say *art* because every teacher brings a style and approach to the classroom that is unique.

The new teacher will read these pages looking for ideas that have proven successful in the classroom. Seasoned teachers will use the ideas expressed within this book to validate their techniques or to expand and improve their approach.

As you read, you will discover that Mr. Sgambato is dedicated to a student-centered classroom approach. He is a firm believer that you must create an environment that allows the student to perform with a high level of self-confidence. His methods and lessons, as he has presented them in this book, have proven highly effective.

I believe that Mr. Sgambato's message is, *If you are well-prepared, student centered, and comfortable in your own skin, then you will experience the Joys of Teaching.*

Walt Wheeler
Retired school principal and
former adjunct professor with
the University of Phoenix

Preface

As a professional teacher, you undoubtedly enjoy immersing your students in daily lessons. What if you could encourage even greater academic passion, interact with them even more successfully, and be extraordinarily influential in touching their futures? The contents of this book will help you to increase your effectiveness in dealing with your students. It is a collection of unconventional classroom approaches, lessons, and strategies rarely found in text form. They serve to:

- successfully acquire your students' undivided attention,
- strongly influence a sincere appreciation for their education and motivation to learn, and
- creatively inspire their thought processes in a variety of successful, academic ventures.

They work!

My intended audience includes any professional educator engaged in this grand vocation with a desire to motivate and educate one's students while simultaneously appreciating the adventure of effectively communicating with our young.

One of my main objectives is to offer personal advice with suggestions utilizing appropriate educational strategies. Of equal importance is the book's recommendation of ways to build strong relationships of respect and trust with your students, while utilizing stimulating methods of academic and personal communication designed to captivate attention and motivate a sincere desire to learn. Numerous techniques designed to accomplish these objectives are found within.

Today's students are graduating into a world of unprecedented change filled with challenges that necessitate unique and inspiring scholastic skills on the part of their teachers. Many of our present educational styles and approaches demand appropriate modifications, developed in a manner so as to vigorously motivate our pupils. Standard techniques frequently waste time and bar progress, leaving many of our kids short of reaching potential academic success, as well as remaining unaware of education's true benefits.

Chapters within offer practical advice and stimulating, educational concepts. The approaches contain inspiring, unorthodox techniques that will encourage your students to sincerely appreciate the advantages of your academic efforts.

Additional information within this book has been designed to inspire and encourage teachers in viewing their professional lives, their teaching responsibilities, and especially their students in a unique, exciting, and thankful manner. The content also stresses the significant potential of the average adolescent. It is vital that educators consider their pupils' general behavior and views of life at these sometimes difficult ages, as well as some of the astonishing achievements attained when they are given the opportunities.

Beginning this investigative educational journey is a chapter entitled "Joys of Teaching." What better way to launch the excursion than reading evidence reminding you of the many delights derived from your chosen career.

Acknowledgments

This book was made possible by the support, encouragement, and guidance of the following colleagues: Mike Gifford, Tom Murray, Walt Wheeler, Carol Edwards, Myrna Herb, Kurt Fetter, Gretta Smith, Carol Green, Maryanne Brookman, and Jeanne DeValve.

Mike and Tom, the two gentlemen at the top of the list, were in a position to provide me with a remarkably generous amount of patience, honesty, and amazing assistance. The information contained within the book would not measure up nearly as well as it does without them. Tom and Mike, thank you so much for your gracious time and support.

Walt Wheeler is formerly our school principal, adjunct professor with the University of Phoenix, author of my book's foreword, and a good friend. Thank you for your ongoing support, patience, and useful advice throughout my teaching career and during the construction of this book.

And lastly, a heartfelt thank-you to all the wonderful young people who entered my life for thirty-five years. I cannot imagine having done anything else for a living. As Harvey Mackay (motivational speaker and author) stated, "If you love your job, you never work a day in your life."

Introduction

What is a teacher's most important responsibility? Many would respond, "*Instruction of curricula.*" Though a mastery of one's curricula is, indeed, essential to teaching, the most important commitment for educators is effective *interaction* with students. Nothing works more powerfully in bringing about a sincere appreciation of their education along with the incentive to *acquire knowledge*. Successful interaction *paves the way* for learning. This book's main purpose is to help accomplish exactly this.

There are approximately 3 million public school teachers in classrooms today, with an additional 310,000 entering the profession yearly. Most would agree that they can certainly use valuable classroom suggestions.

The interior contains nine chapters within four sections:

1. *You* Retain the Potential to Inspire, Motivate, and Support Your Students
2. Professional Advice for Dealing with Your Students
3. Tools That Succeed: Unconventional Approaches and Strategies
4. Is There More That We Can Do?

A closer look.

PART I: *YOU* RETAIN THE POTENTIAL TO INSPIRE, MOTIVATE, AND SUPPORT YOUR STUDENTS

Included are descriptions of *joys* experienced within the world of education that will emotionally move the reader to familiar depths of professional gratification and pride in being a teacher.

The accounts are designed to encourage a recollection of your own poignant episodes in the classroom, thus reminding you of the splendid delight enjoyed as well as your potential influence upon the many students encountered in your career. The chapters are filled with examples of the ways teachers inspire, motivate, and support their students.

The professional joys you obtain help underscore your role in possessing the potential to positively affect the many students who enter your arena of instruction. Reflect upon your formidable role and potential influence while considering the endless possibility of significant, sensitive episodes yet to be experienced within your career.

PART II: PROFESSIONAL ADVICE FOR DEALING WITH YOUR STUDENTS

This section contains personal advice to consider when spending so much of your life in the classroom. Offered are suggestions supporting effective ways to build strong connections of respect and trust with your students. This step is essential prior to entering the arena of today's educational challenges. If you are following the *Common Core Standards*, then these proposals will be immensely useful in getting your students on board.

PART III: TOOLS THAT SUCCEED: UNCONVENTIONAL APPROACHES AND STRATEGIES

A collection of unique lessons, approaches, and professional strategies containing inspiring, unorthodox, and very effective educational components. These unconventional methods serve to acquire the students' undivided attention; influence their desire to learn as well as their self-esteem; and creatively motivate their thought processes in a variety of successful, academic ventures.

The *preparatory lessons* included within chapters 6 and 7 ("Cooperative Classroom Environment" and "The Seat of Distinction") have a common purpose. Their intention is to blend the students into an effective team possessing common goals while learning within a collaborative setting. The result is a group of youngsters with a shared understanding of their roles, responsibilities, and the determination to work together successfully. These molding activities function as time-saving investments for the remainder of the year.

Classroom obstructions, disagreements, misbehaviors, withdrawals, displays of anger, and lack of effort are more easily avoided. By successfully grooming your students—coaching and preparing them for their nine and one-half months in your classroom—precious time is saved. Educational experiences blend together more easily and move along more successfully. A greater possibility will exist that the students will be on the same page as their teacher. You're not wasting time in offering these activities. You're being conscientious and better organized.

PART IV: IS THERE MORE THAT WE CAN DO?

Two chapters offering unconventional lessons and projects suggesting ways for your students to:

- help other class members experience opportunities to meet with success;
- express genuine feelings and discuss emotional issues while building confidence and self-esteem;
- experience pride and self-respect, as well as a clear perception of their own potential value;
- determine ways to avoid insecurity, low self-esteem, anger, and violence; and
- enhance multicultural acceptance, counter the existence of bigotry, and work together in understanding, accepting, and celebrating different cultural traditions.

In chapters 8 and 9, several exclusive projects are described. They easily have the potential to provide valuable lifetime learning experiences and rewarding results for many of today's young people. These unique encounters offer an abundance of evidence as to what these youngsters can successfully comprehend as well as achieve.

An added benefit: Effective classroom lessons appear within several chapters. They include all procedure details used in their development. The reader is asked to initially read the descriptions in their entirety. If, at a later time, one wishes to engage the shorter, formatted "lesson plan" version, then it exists within the appendix.

Part I

YOU RETAIN THE POTENTIAL TO INSPIRE, MOTIVATE, AND SUPPORT YOUR STUDENTS

Chapter One

Joys of Teaching

JOY NO. 1: CONTACT WITH FORMER STUDENTS

"Mr. Johnson, remember me? Joanne Freeman? You were my seventh-grade math teacher!"

From time to time, educators have the pleasure of making contact with former students. This could be through classroom visits or when unexpectedly meeting individuals who were members of a particular class two, six, ten, or more years ago. If you've been in the profession for several years or longer, this has more than likely already occurred. When fortunate enough to experience these occasions, it no doubt pleases you that you're remembered—but what may give you even more satisfaction is when these young people recall something you did or said that they found themselves fondly remembering.

If they share such an incident with you, then you may find yourself caught off guard, even stumbling for words, ultimately saying, "Thank you," as you attempt to let the individual know just how meaningful the experience is. No matter how difficult a day you may be having, regardless how stressed you may be feeling, these encounters will quickly remind you of the grand rewards reaped from this delightful profession.

JOY OF TEACHING NO. 2: THE "TEACHER RUSH"

When was the last time you experienced the "Teacher Rush"—that moment when that *something special* happens in your lesson? You may lead students in a stimulating class conversation ending with an unexpected conclusion or reveal a surprising detail about a particular subject. Heads turn, eyes lift and sparkle, the room goes silent, students stare, all eyes are upon you. And you know they're doing some heavy thinking—and most significantly, it was *you* who made them think! What a feeling! It's as though some kind of *magic* has occurred.

The *magic* is part of teaching. It lives in your classroom. There's a way to access the phenomenon, re-experiencing and appreciating the sensation again: After a long day of teaching, stop at the door for a moment before exiting. (It works best when the building is quiet.) There is an essence of classroom magic that you can encounter again. Begin by looking around the room, slowly, taking in the walls, bulletin boards, desks, chairs.

Then focus on the hands that were in the air; the stares; the questions; the comments; the enthusiasm; the laughter; the expressions on the faces of young people who had, at earlier moments of the day, perhaps discovered something about math, science, English, home and career skills, social studies, technology, physical education, health or Spanish, that they found interesting, challenging, *different.* And *you* held their eyes, their attention, their interest, their education, perhaps even a small part of their future, in your hands for a brief time. The room may be empty, but you can still perceive the phenomenon. The magic is there. Just take the time before leaving to recall, to reminisce, to *feel.*

We are given the opportunity to live on this planet for many reasons—foremost in importance, being of service to others. That's why many of us find ourselves in education. It's a wonderful way to satisfy that opportunity. "If you love your job, you never *work* a day in your life"—a phrase popularized by business writer Harvey Mackay that is certainly applicable.

The late Arthur Ashe said, "From what we get, we can make a living; what we give, however, makes a life." You've entered one of the noblest professions—and you've succeeded; you're a *teacher.* You've touched many lives; your influence has spread. You deserve to be proud.

JOY OF TEACHING NO. 3: INSPIRE YOUR STUDENTS

How? What's the best way?

Involve them in the lesson—preferably by using a prepared, unconventional approach. If a teacher can acquire students' total attention and gain their sincere interest, then it's likely that all will be moving side by side in the same academic direction—and everyone will share the enjoyment.

Involving your students entails more than simply listening to the teacher. It requires them to become totally *immersed, committed, absorbed,* and *determined* in the lesson. Certainly, cooperative learning is an effective way to begin, or you could use any other well-devised approach to attract and immediately engage the kids. Be creative in *hooking* them into the lesson. Then, with a plan of *immersed* involvement in mind, you can design lessons to encourage large amounts of peer interaction among the students, breaking them into teams of two, perhaps, while encouraging discussions centered on the task at hand.

After the teams discuss the subject and find potential directions to pursue in resolving the task, combine each team with another unit of two and direct them to continue the dialogue as they develop additional information and individual opinions. Following this segment, engage in a *community meeting* involving the entire class.

Within this setting, encourage dialogue to transpire as the group considers numerous solutions and opinions in pursuing the theme. Because of their personal involvement, they become more strongly focused on the lesson. With this approach, not only do students make academic progress, but they also develop more positive, cooperative social skills and build self-confidence. It works much better than a didactic lecture stemming solely from the teacher.

When young people talk together, they learn together and, consequently, progress together. Watch as the room fills with comments dealing with the task at hand. Enjoy the expressions, gestures, and involvement.

> Tell me and I forget . . .
> Show me, and I remember . . .
> Involve me, and I learn![1]
> (Supported by research)

This approach encourages *active student involvement*: Within a unique, comfortable environment, your students will achieve security, reassurance, and motivation, which can usher in more active scholastic dialogue and progress.

A secure, relaxed setting more easily:

- builds small-group trust and support;
- introduces a *group process* of working together;

- increases awareness of self and others;
- increases communication, active listening, and trust;
- bridges gaps among genders, personalities, temperaments, and so on;
- involves everyone;
- builds supportive groups to prevent aberrant behavior (loneliness, rejection, negative peer pressure, failure, tension); and
- inspires.

Involve them—they will learn.
Additional suggestions:

- How about one or two students, with your guidance, taking a *chunk* of a future lesson and actually teaching it? Yes, they can! With a team approach and sufficient preparation time, a group can quite easily acquire a formidable comprehension of a topic. It will reinforce their knowledge, not to mention involve the rest of the class in a successfully unique and entertaining approach. The whole idea could academically motivate the other class members, especially if they, too, will be taking on a lesson responsibility.

LEARNING PYRAMID

Average Retention Rate

Level	Rate
LECTURE	5%
READING	10%
AUDIO-VISUAL	20%
DEMONSTRATION	30%
DISCUSSION GROUP	50%
PRACTICE BY DOING	75%
TEACH OTHERS/IMMEDIATE USE OF LEARNING	90%

National Training Laboratories Bethel, Maine

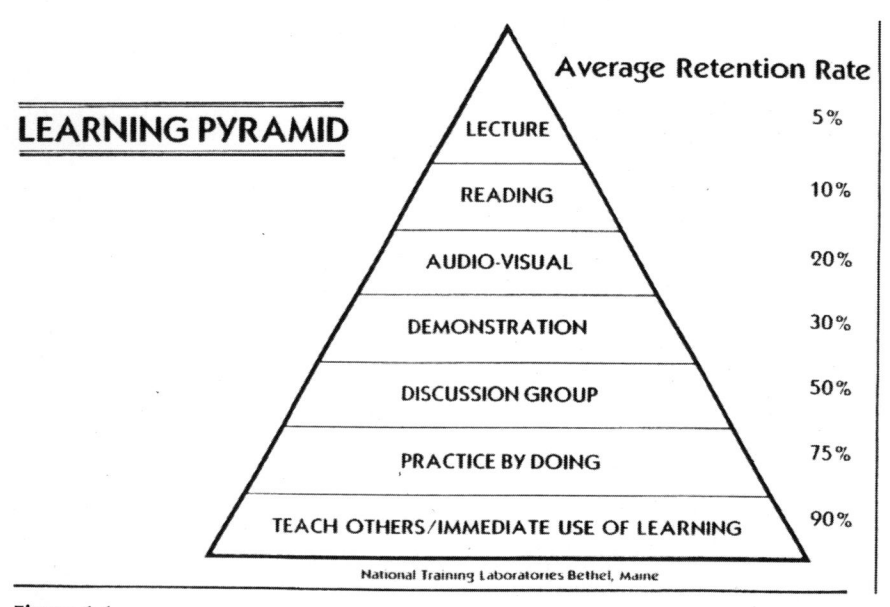

Figure 1.1

- How about videotaping them as they teach, having the class view it, and then perhaps passing the recording onto other classrooms? Possibly devise other methods to involve them in an unconventional way.
- To back up the proposal of totally involving your students in the lessons, the following information is offered regarding retention rates among students: "Teaching Styles: Consider the Learning Pyramid" developed by the National Training Labs in Bethel, Maine.

Where are you and your students found on the "Learning Pyramid" (fig. 1.1)?

JOY OF TEACHING NO. 4: SINCERE INFLUENCE AND CONCERN

Without warning, you notice that a working student appears troubled, stressed, and anxious. You approach her desk and speak to her softly, offering helpful suggestions. Looking into her eyes and putting your hand tenderly on her shoulder, you pause and conclude with, "I know you can do it." She smiles, glows a bit, and then—she does it.

You spent extra time with him working over a mathematical problem, reconstructing a paragraph, or possibly explaining a class assignment. You were happy to do it; you felt helpful. Then, you went on about your business and focused on it no longer. The next day, you spot him as the two of you pass in the corridor. You smile and say hello. He's looking at you differently, however. It's not just the smile or the stare. It's that he obviously did not forget about the time you spent together.

You displayed reassuring comfort to her, a word of caution, perhaps, or plain, simple advice. The event concluded. She thanked you and moved on through the day, through the year, through her life. Will you remember the event in twenty-four hours, twenty-four years? Will *she*?

You may not have the slightest idea as to the nature of an event experienced ten, twenty, thirty years prior, nor what advice you'd given her. However, continue to keep in mind that teachers cannot be fully aware of their potential influence or the length of time students remember their classroom encounters. You may not recall an event, but they surprisingly may. Incredible and so emotionally moving.

JOY OF TEACHING NO. 5: PLANTING SEEDS

How many seeds have you planted? How often have former students moved through their academic years into adulthood thinking of you or mentioning something experienced in your academic arena? How frequently did their thoughts flow back to an event that they shared with you?

If you are unable to enjoy occasional encounters with them, then you might not be aware of these pleasant memories. Rest assured, however, that they did occur. Your students grow up, remembering. They remember *you*.

Are you a *new* teacher, a midcareer teacher, or a teacher near retirement? What motivated you to enter the profession? What is it that the classroom offers you? If you are doing in life what you were meant to do, if you indeed enjoy teaching, then you, more than likely, have your own relevant response to this question readily available.

While engaged in this grand profession, you have the advantage of being of supreme service in a most satisfying way—touching the futures of countless young people as they live their lives. You retain the potential to educate, to influence, to motivate, to persuade. You offer a lesson of interest, a supportive comment, a gesture, a look, a touch—none of which you may remember with the passing of only a few minutes; the young recipients of your encouragement, however, may be able to easily recall the experience and resulting emotions years from that day.

What you say, how you say it, how you dress, how you smile, *if* you smile—we can never be totally certain how our interaction with these young people will ultimately affect their education, inspirations, moods, abilities to persevere, capacities to find comfort in who they truly are—but there is *always* that powerful potential to do so. Plant your seeds.

JOY OF TEACHING NO. 6: NOSTALGIA

You come across a folder, booklet, file, or envelope containing mementos representing many of the wonderful things that happened to you during part of your career. As you peruse the contents, the memories come flooding back. You're still; you become a bit lost in an event that occurred years ago, your eyes blur—how wonderful is the nostalgic ecstasy. Keep the file safely set aside for those occasions when you have a tough day. Then seek the mementos again, and feel comforted.

Chapter Two

Fellowship
The Feel of Support

Arrive at school by 7:45. Work at your profession, and get the job done. Leave no later than 3:30. As you walk down the corridor, bid your goodbyes. "See you Monday."

Anything missing?

How well do you know your colleagues? Is it important for you to truly *know* them? Do you gather? How could teachers ever find time to *gather*? They have enough to do. And besides, they work together professionally; it isn't as though they have to be buddies, right? Please keep reading.

When teachers who are educational colleagues take the opportunity to enhance relationships, they cannot help benefiting. They come to better know each other both professionally and personally. There does not have to be a deliberate effort to bring about camaraderie, fellowship, or personal encouragement among colleagues. No one needs to design a plan aimed at developing a system of support and companionship for your faculty. The benefits may simply transpire.

You may find that you merely enjoy each other's company and sometimes need a friend nearby to listen to your stories, concerns, or perhaps provide recommendations and assistance regarding students' concerns. Personal advice and support can easily be available. Many of these conversations would, naturally, take place following the school day.

Admittedly, the further one travels to work, the less likely one is to spend additional time in the school building after hours. The rewards obtained, however, often make the expenditure of time well worth the investment.

Comingling is an important factor in working together, supporting each other, and striving for excellence. Who benefits? *Everyone*, especially the students. No matter what the kids' needs are, frequent positive interaction among the entire staff makes the deliverance of those necessities that much more likely and occur with greater haste.

The transition from professional to casual acquaintance may prove to be a rewarding experience. Sharing time, backgrounds, goals, cocktails, and especially laughter exposes participants to other dimensions of their colleagues' personalities. Stronger connections transpire. And, even if members don't always agree on topics pursued, they advance as professionals, as individuals, and as a faculty. There is a greater tendency for the group to move forward together, arms interlocked, focused on the same goal.

Though you may have developed different teaching styles, they could be placed aside when it comes time for more important educational pursuits. Yes, you are teachers; you may also, however, become better acquainted and, consequently, develop closer relationships—and friends you may certainly remain.

Part II

PROFESSIONAL ADVICE FOR DEALING WITH YOUR STUDENTS

Chapter Three

Learning from Classroom Experience

Four years of college, education courses, observations, student teaching, bachelor's degree in teaching! Perhaps even a master's! Totally ready!

Well, maybe.

Or maybe not.

What else could possibly help tailor a teacher's proficiency in the classroom?

The only thing missing, of course, is experiential wisdom: that which is learned through extensive classroom involvement. There are, obviously, no courses available. These are the skills usually acquired through years of on-the-job encounters.

This chapter, however, will be of help. Whether you're totally new to the classroom or on the job for a number of years, consider the following suggestions. Ultimately, they may boost your skills, improve relationships, and save you time.

Misbehavior is not restricted only to boys; girls may participate as well. Each of the examples that follow, however, will often abstain from using both male-female pronouns "he/she" simply for reasons of reading simplicity.

LEARNING FROM EXPERIENCE NO. 1: SUPPORT AND EMPATHY

Is a student apt to do better academically if she perceives your genuine concern for her welfare? No question; a teacher's sincerity and compassion are important tools of the teaching profession. They don't need to be planned, prepared, and released. They are required, however, to be offered by the teacher and observed by the student. If you allow your desires of support and empathy to manifest, they can then be perceived by your pupil.

The youngster who is easily intimidated when called upon to answer questions or asked to participate in class needs to *feel* your encouragement through your demeanor, eye contact, body language, nearness, choice of terminology, and sometimes even gentleness.

The instructor needn't *prepare* these behaviors. One must simply *permit* them to be expressed, to surface in one's approach. The message of patience, understanding, and concern is then conveyed. Once the student successfully interprets the teacher's willingness to help, she may be encouraged to try, to work harder, to maintain a higher level of attentiveness and energy in achieving success in the classroom. So if you like kids and you love teaching, it's easy. Just be yourself, allowing her to perceive your sincerity. The student will likely grow in confidence and give it her best.

LEARNING FROM EXPERIENCE NO. 2: RESPECT

What are your feelings as you enter the classroom? Are you all business? Do you focus strongly on discipline? Do you enter the *world of your students* and engage? Is there time for humor in your lesson? Is *respect* important? Respect for whom? Would this be students' respect for the teacher or the teacher's respect for the students? The answer is *yes* to both.

A teacher once commented, "They *must* respect me; I am their teacher, an adult. If they want *my* respect, however, they must *earn* it." The attitude is coarse, unrealistic, and self-defeating. Truthfully, many students will not remember the subject matter you taught. A few may even forget your particular grade level. Nearly all, however, will remember how you treated them and what they *derived from the relationship*. Why not take advantage of your position to model respect? This would encourage the student to feel accepted, as though he will be treated fairly and honestly. And when many of these youngsters view respect displayed by the teacher, they are more inclined to incorporate the behavior within their own lives.

Remember, it is the environmentally comfortable student who is usually more willing to take on academic responsibilities throughout the year. Your display of *respect* need not be exaggerated. Allow it to develop naturally; an amicable, respectful teacher stands a greater chance of persuading young people to follow. Respect for students equates to an extended hand followed by the words "Come with me on this journey."

Some of the most important things we teach may be our intrinsic values. We don't have to put them into words. All we have to do is live them. We become existing examples, hopefully displaying empathy, patience, respect, understanding, tolerance, dignity—and a sense of humor. Without question, it's a presentation of your personal values that makes up a large part of what you'll be teaching your students.

LEARNING FROM EXPERIENCE NO. 3: DON'T LET THEM HIDE

You, no doubt, have already experienced it. Some young people frequently feel a need to conceal their natural feelings, thoughts, or moods by attempting to hide behind averted glances or eyes that roll to the ceiling, even looks of defiance. Though they are unwilling to admit this, even to themselves, some are quite proficient in the behavior.

So what can you do? Let them *see who you are*. If you move in closer to the individuals and offer a sincere, receptive expression, you may more easily succeed in capturing their attention. Consequently, they will have difficulty preventing you from reading their eyes. It isn't necessary to remain in close proximity for lengthy periods, only long enough to make an open, friendly offer. You'll know them better; they'll know you better. Keep in mind that this may not be achieved the *first* time you engage the technique.

LEARNING FROM EXPERIENCE NO. 4: UNCONVENTIONAL DISCIPLINE AND SECOND-ORDER CHANGE

"Stop that!" "Sit down!" "I said, sit down!" "Please keep quiet!" "Stop it!" "Stop it right now!" "I'm not going to tell you again!" "I said, sit down!" "I'm waiting!" "I'm not going to tell you again!"

These outbursts may work at first. Then, however, many students grow used to hearing orders delivered in the same manner and, consequently, may more easily ignore them. Many teachers too often continue using the same attempts at disciplining the kids. The result: The efforts are less and less effective, to say the least. That is a result of *first-order change* (using the *same* unsuccessful methods in attempting to obtain *different* behavior).

When attempting to affect students' conduct while using first-order change, one ends up doing and saying the same things over and over again. The result? Behavior is unchanged. That's because *the teacher's* behavior is unchanged.

In *second-order change*, the teacher alters what he says and does in order to strongly influence a change in behavior. The philosophy: Do it differently, even be a bit unorthodox. Try not to use anger, threats, volume, or any other disengaging tactics.[2]

Advice: Do not approach the arena of discipline in the manner anticipated by the student. Approach in a *unique* fashion. It saves time, works better, and avoids unpleasant results. Take a closer look at what is being suggested:

One of the most successful obstructions in preventing a teacher's perceptive ability to read a student's true intention is the kid's "anger block." Now you, of course, are the adult, the teacher, the one in charge. However, sometimes it's necessary for the teacher to step back, allowing the emotional situation to *deescalate*. Be patient and allow the state of affairs to settle a bit. Look for an opportunity, possibly a short time later, to approach the student in a milder manner to talk, clarify, and guide him, offering evidence that you are not his enemy.

This could be done during study hall, after school, or even on an occasion after stepping into the corridor to engage in a conversation concerning his disruptive behavior, demand for attention, or intrusion on the teacher's class time. The trip into the corridor, though not the most ideal tactic to employ, may be, on occasion, the only recourse available. It may have been apparent to the entire class, of course, that he's *misbehaved*, he's *wrong*. His response to your *invitation* to leave the classroom for a chat was a shaking of his head, perhaps a hard push on the desk while sliding his chair back and a defiant glare in his eyes.

Once in the hall, he's expecting your demeaning words, your volume, your criticism—first-order change. Instead of immediately scolding him through your own expression of anger, how about beginning slowly, with something unexpected like, "Your two buddies, Frankie and Peter, must think that I'm yelling at you. Yep, I can see them staring at the door, nodding with expressions of certainty"? Second-order change.

His defiant glare may not melt away, but don't let that stop you. He most likely is trying to figure out what is happening. Meanwhile, his anger may be unexpectedly taking a *backseat* (de-escalation is beginning to occur). Remember, your de-escalating approach is totally up to you to devise; just avoid immediate comments of disapproval and annoyance.

At that point, with nonthreatening body posture and volume, proceed to explain to him, from an honest, personal point of view, why you need everyone's attention. What he's doing is costing you time, and once the time is lost, you usually can't make it up. Though you know of everyone's need for attention, loss of class time is unfair to *all* the students in the class as well as to you. *You* are the teacher with a responsibility to *teach*. Your obligation is important. Engage his eyes and explain it in your own manner, without employing a harsh tone.

Though he may somewhat retain a look of anger, his brain may have begun to view his teacher in a totally new and unexpected way. He sees, perhaps, more of who you truly are. You spoke to him firmly but with honesty, patience, and even a bit of respect. He may not easily forget this engagement. Yes, you could very well be making a rare and lasting impression.

Then, to top it off, why not ask if he'd like to slowly walk by the door window to check out Frankie and Peter's behavior? Just as he begins to move, however, offer, "Whatever you do, don't smile." This adds a slight touch of humor but, more importantly, an offer to *share* the moment, ridding the scene of a "teacher reprimanding student" theme. Following that, continue the discussion, seeking to determine if he truly understands your genuine intention. Use what you've learned about his personality to deal with the situation.

Now, do you actually have the time and freedom to step into the hall? It depends, of course, on the circumstances. Keep in mind that most of this scene could very well take place at the end of the school day, in private.

Will this always work? Perhaps not. (Would you be satisfied if it worked most of the time?) Can you use it with every student? In each case, you would have to be the judge. At times, you will need to rely on more conventional teacher-type responses. However, if possible:

- allow deescalation of emotion to take place and
- employ an unorthodox approach when necessary; it gets their attention more easily and has greater potential of retaining their cooperation.

Please keep in mind: During adolescence, kids begin experiencing unfamiliar changes in their bodies *and* in their feelings. Many sense an impression of being misunderstood as they struggle out of childhood and into the world of adults. While attempting to wriggle free of their juvenile existence, they often engage defiant behaviors, disobedience, disrespect, sibling rivalry, lying, cheating, academic problems, negative attitudes, peer pressure, and depression. Teachers need to keep this in mind when dealing with them.

Got a kid staying after school? Will you sit behind your desk, working, as your pupil quietly sits, waiting to be dismissed, or will you consider the time an opportunity to make progress in helping him view the classroom differently and obtaining his cooperation? How can this youngster be approached in a way that will harness his attention, promote discussion, provide an opportunity for him to perceive your sincere concern and see you as a person with his best interests in mind? Remove the barrier! Grab a chair (not too close; don't intimidate), and start to pursue a dialogue.

Possible conversation starters:

- "Steve, didn't I see you at last Friday's game? Did the score surprise you?"
- "Steve, what would you be doing if you weren't here?"
- "What is the worst part about our school?"
- "What is the best part about our school?"

Progress toward greater seriousness and sincerity. The answer to the last question may very well be, "The bell at the end of eighth period." Fine. Don't criticize his responses. Ask *why*. Continue with conversation. Additional suggestions for initiating conversation include the following:

- "What do you see yourself doing ten years from today?"
- "What is the best thing that could happen to you?"
- "If you could change one thing about our school, what would it be?"
- "How would you change it?"
- "If you could change one thing about yourself, what would it be?"

Just start it. Get a conversation going. You don't have to have a secure, detailed plan. Read the kid's mind a bit. Think back: Who are his friends? What types of behavior does he find amusing? What does his T-shirt say? Does it state the name of a band or sports team? Are you familiar with it? Use this information to your advantage in initiating a conversation.

There are times when a seemingly insignificant exchange or engagement occurs between teacher and student that redirects the relationship in a new and positive way. As an example, suppose a student commits a behavior *infraction* for which he must be *retained* following the school day. Let's say that you've approached him and explained in a nonthreatening but firm manner that you will be in your room, waiting for him after the last period. Prepare your simple plan:

After entering your room at the end of the day, allow him to quietly sit for a time (as he, perhaps, pretends to read a novel). Then, verbally approach him in an unexpected manner: Bring up a recent sports event, musical concert, humorous event, or even sad event of which you're both aware—anything totally unrelated to school or his misbehavior. He will most likely be somewhat restrained in conversation at first but continue nevertheless.

If you've chosen an appropriate topic, he will eventually show increasing interest, and comments will occur more frequently. This helps to build or rebuild the relationship as well as sets a more appropriate foundation for what's to follow.

The next step would be to quietly and nonoffensively direct his attention to his misbehavior, followed with something like, "Here's my message, Tom. Something was obviously bothering you. However, I don't think it was resolved by your yelling and walking out of the room this morning. The kids thought you were acting strangely. It began your day with a huge negative feeling, and you're ending the day with an extra forty-five minutes in school instead of joining your friends for some fun. Tom, I'm not upset because of what you did to me; I'm upset because of what you did to *you.*" Give him time to emotionally absorb what you've said. He will, more than likely, sense your sincere concern over his welfare. Then, discuss his reasons for the outburst and offer suggestions as to what he can do the next time he experiences similar feelings.

Do not be surprised on the following day if he should seem more settled, content, smiling, and willing to engage your academic work. You did not use first-order change; you were totally different, unconventional, as you worked your way into his personality and behaved in an unorthodox manner to which he could relate. Your interest in his well-being was obvious. You were on his side and there, he perceived, you will remain.

Remember, the important thing is to be different, creative, untraditional, even a bit peculiar—not what they are expecting. Find unconventional approaches that match your personality. Treating these youngsters in the usual, expected manner will provide positive results with many. However, the teacher who can use unpredictable and unconventional methods with a "difficult" kid or situation stands a much better chance of getting the attention of even more adolescents, as well as nurturing their compliance.

LEARNING FROM EXPERIENCE NO. 5: IT'S *YOUR* RESPONSIBILITY

Butch is talking out of turn again. He's done it three times during this period alone. Time is going by, and you need to proceed with the lesson. The only alternative is to remove Butch from class, enabling you to remain on track and complete the lesson, right? *Send him to the principal's office.* There—problem solved!

Nope: The problem is *larger.* Butch will more than likely return to your room on the next day (or in some cases, during the same period following his "talk with the principal"). He is *your* student. He is *your* responsibility. Removing the kid speaks volumes to the class, especially to *him.* Your actions may very well be interpreted as: "Mr. Johnston can't handle Butch. Butch got his way. He received the attention from us that he loves. He got out of working in class" or "Everybody watched as *I* interrupted the class."

You absolutely must take some kind of action, but the plan must already be in existence. The strategy needs to be prepared beforehand. You've no doubt observed the kid in the past; you know what he's capable of doing.

Develop your counter-design, and have it ready. Why not develop your plan two months before school begins, just in case you need it?

Not sure what to do? Ask a mentor, the guidance counselor, or a colleague you've observed who appears to be well-seasoned, relaxed, friendly, and willing to help. Call the guy you had as a seventh-grade math teacher who had no difficulty with discipline. Whatever you do, don't simply send him to the office! (Don't forget: Whatever you covered with the class while he was gone, you'll have to teach him.)

LEARNING FROM EXPERIENCE NO. 6: THE TEACHER'S ARENA

What is your favorite location in your classroom? From where do you instruct your students? The least effective location: "From my desk." Do *you* simply stand or sit in the "Teacher's Arena" near your desk or in your chair while addressing your class? This could easily put you on a different level, at a different frequency—miles away from your students' world.

Sitting behind the desk or standing near it especially limits your ability to maintain the class's attention; appear approachable; exhibit body language and expression; display excitement; maintain control; perceive students' moods; and, last but certainly not least, enjoy teaching. If you truly needed to sit for a short time, choose a different location. Sit on a table corner, windowsill, student's desk, the sink—anyplace but the *teacher's chair*. The proper response to the question should be, "Wherever I need to be in order to achieve my goals."

LEARNING FROM EXPERIENCE NO. 7: WATCH YOUR LANGUAGE

No, the topic is not obscenities. Rather, employ not only classroom-appropriate dialogue but also words and phrases that work in an optimistic, encouraging manner for your students. Using words and phrases that do not motivate in a positive, sincere fashion (the *wrong language*) could imply to them a lack of concern, a sense of disenchantment, dismissiveness, and superiority.

Using the right language projects a sense of interest, sincerity, attentiveness, and respect. This doesn't mean that you need to start collecting a resource of new vocabulary words; it does imply, however, that you prepare a thought process, reminding yourself of your position, your responsibility, and the possibility of your influencing these kids in a positive manner.

Let's look at positive reinforcement. When a student hands in an impressive assignment or answers a difficult question correctly, you may be tempted to simply reply, "Good job!" Fine. Use it *once* per class, even once per month; that's it! To the ears of many adolescents, a response begins to lose sincerity, significance, and power when they hear the same words again and again, especially from the same individual. Consequently, they may not feel as verbally rewarded. The same goes for any other phrases that seem to be shared by far too many parents and educators, such as, "Good answer," "That a boy!," and so on.

How about an encouraging response that truly gets a pupil's attention and makes the kid feel sincerely, verbally compensated:

- "I am impressed!"
- "I call that progress!"
- "I like the way you handled that!"
- "Thank you, thank you!"
- "Maybe you should be up here, and I should be sitting there."
- "Great, my friend."
- "Super!"
- "Man, are you on the right track!"
- "You make me look good!"
- "I am proud of you."

Be *original*; be sincere. *Yes*, it does make a difference!
And speaking of language usage, read on.

LEARNING FROM EXPERIENCE NO. 8: "OK"

When it's time for the active class discussion to conclude or the kids must line up at the door in preparation for the field trip or everyone must give you their attention for anything, what word(s) do you use in obtaining their attention? Is it *OK*—over and over, on every occasion?

Does *OK* become boring, obsolete, and less significant to the kids after they've heard it from the majority of teachers year after year? Does it continually work well in getting a quick response? Want to increase the lack of attention? Just say, "OK!" Can you find another word or words? You can? OK!

LEARNING FROM EXPERIENCE NO. 9: CLARITY

When in front of the class, taking on your professional responsibilities, try not to *announce* the beginning of the lesson. You need, of course, to explain the direction of the session, but do not allow your students to become accustomed to a loud declaration on your part, indicating that you wish them to quiet down. Rather, stand in front of the class in your *instructor's pose*. If necessary, stare at anyone still engaged in conversation. Let them see that following the bell, you're ready to begin.

Do not raise your voice in competition with other noise in the classroom. The interpretation may be that you don't mind a vocal challenge, that they are permitted to converse until the teacher increases his or her volume. If you allow them to wait for the "shout," then they'll more easily assume that they may take the time to complete the conversation prior to listening to the lesson's beginning. Once assuming the *instructor's pose* and acquiring their attention, pause for a few seconds as your eyes sweep back and forth across the room using the *teacher stare*. This will help *fixate* their attention.

LEARNING FROM EXPERIENCE NO. 10: LESSON PLANS

Are daily lesson plans truly necessary? A teacher once insisted that daily lesson plans are, in fact, a "waste of time. I know what I'm doing. I've been doing the same thing for nearly ten years!" exclaimed the individual.

Really? And the daily progress has been exactly the same with each class for all ten years? Additionally, has the nature of motivation for each group also been the same, along with the guided practice, assignments, organizing skills, attention, and recall? Is this reality?

The instructor needs to consider the ability of each class, to focus on its progress since the unit was begun and the type of inspirational stimuli required, not to mention also spend quality time creating the perfect strategies to gain the students' attention and interest.

Developing the lesson, absorbing it, modifying it, tweaking it; the plan must be firmly embedded within your brain before you approach the students with it. Are daily lesson plans truly necessary? Absolutely! And what are the tools used to build the lesson?

The labeled tools for lesson construction may differ, depending on when and where you attended college. Whether a teacher employs the terms *anticipatory set, introduction, motivation, hook, main lesson, development, procedure, closure,* or *conclusion* is not of primary importance. However, a lesson is made up of a beginning, a middle, and an end. And that is what a good teacher needs in formulating a successful experience for a class of young people.

This is not to say, however, that each period requires a full *plan sheet* displaying paragraphs of information. Short phrases and simple "reminding words" in a plan book displaying a full week's program of lessons, notes, and activities are fine. If a constructed lesson develops into a larger intricate plan, write down any short necessary components to keep in hand, on your desk, or on a podium for reference.

Would you like to hold on to your plan book so as to possibly include some of the same components for next year? Absolutely! However, we'll assume that modifications may possibly be necessary.

When the teacher develops lesson plans, he or she:

- is able to rely on the organization of a written set of prepared strategies;
- has the option of reviewing the lesson's motivation, progress, homework assigned, modifications, and so on;
- has a more precise idea of the ultimate goal;
- can view and anticipate the progress through the lesson in a logical order;
- can view every step of the instructional timeline in a clear and easy manner and thus better prepare for the teaching process in advance (this visualization increases teacher success potential);
- can plan more effectively and avoid frustration;
- has the option to modify or improve the lesson's design;

- is better able to achieve objectives;
- has a record of the lesson's progress and components if absent;
- is able to go back and analyze one's own teaching (what went well, what didn't) and then improve on it for its next use; and
- may anticipate the students' questions by reviewing the content.

And remember: Be flexible. The lesson plan is not a set of directions guiding one in installing an oil filter. Things happen. Be prepared.

LEARNING FROM EXPERIENCE NO. 11: THE NEW KID

There's a knock at your classroom door. It's the guidance counselor or the principal or some guy in suit and tie with a smile on his face. Doesn't matter. What *is* important is the fourteen-year-old standing next to him. Yeah, you've already figured it out.

"Good morning, Ms. Farrell. This is Bill Antuda from Nebraska. His family just arrived, and he is entering our school system today. He is an eighth-grader, and I've placed him in your class." *A new student.* Oh, no! It's March. How will you possibly catch him up with the work, especially considering that the curriculum in Nebraska is certainly not the same as in your state?

Yes, it will be your responsibility, and it won't be easy. Let's see, now, how can you *make this event even more difficult?*

- Don't smile at the kid. Just stare at him.
- "Doesn't Mr. Frank have fewer students in *his* class?"
- "How do I deal with this, sir? It's so late in the year?"
- Appear to take a long difficult breath and let your cheeks puff up as you exhale. Then, after pursing your lips, utter, "OK," and return to your room with your new student behind you. Tell him to sit anywhere, leaving the *decision* up to him as to where to *insert* himself. (Hasn't he got enough to deal with?)

The above responses will, of course, not bring about his very best academic effort. It will, quite likely, do just the opposite.

How about this:

Extend your hand to him and say, "Hey, Bill, welcome to Disney World. Nice to meet you. First days can be a bit uncomfortable. However, I think you'll grow to like it here. We've got some great kids. Come, follow me, Bill." Simply do what you can in your own way to extend an element of friendly comfort. Watch his reaction. Not what he was expecting? Good. Can he deal with your wit? If necessary, adjust it.

"Welcome to our school, Bill. Class, this is Bill Antuda. He'll be joining us for the remainder of the year. Bill, have a seat right here. (Seat him quickly.) Joanne, please inform Bill as to what topic we're studying." Dialogue between Bill and Joanne ensues while you briefly get involved in "something" at your desk (allow the "barrier" to be broken). Then, at your first opportunity, corral a trusted student to accompany (lead) the boy to his next class. Between bells, find him. How's he doing?

Interview the kid later. Talk to his parents. Get his records from the office or from Nebraska. Reach out to other professionals for help. There *is* an answer to dealing with the curriculum problem; find it!

LEARNING FROM EXPERIENCE NO. 12:
KEEP TALKING WHILE SHE'S INTERRUPTING

You have the group's attention; things are going well as you progress toward the conclusion to the lesson. All eyes are on you—all eyes except Lori's, that is. She's speaking in a whisper again to Betsy. If you stop, however, to scold or ask for her attention, you suffer a disruption. What can you do to deter her behavior?

My advice: Continue teaching and talking while moving toward her desk. With you standing behind her, she's unlikely to continue the conversation. (If her ears turn red, she is totally aware of your presence and has definitely concluded the conversation.)

Want to be somewhat creative in totally capturing her attention, bringing her back into the fold? After fifteen seconds, direct your words toward a question she can easily answer, and call on her. Try another tactic. Continue teaching, finding a reason within the next minute or so to refer to her earlier contribution; be certain to mention her name, look at her, and point to her. (The second and third steps may not be totally necessary. However, they usually do work well in bringing Lori back into the lesson's direction.) Then continue moving about the room while teaching. When a student appears to lose interest or begins to bother another, walk toward the kid and simply continue.

LEARNING FROM EXPERIENCE NO. 13:
SUCCEED IN YOUR WARNINGS OF ENDANGERMENT

Members of our younger generation are frequently told by adults not to participate in certain perilous behaviors. In order to succeed, however, these kids must be approached in a thought-out, appropriate manner. Too often, that's not what transpires. (Example: "Just say, 'No.'") This approach frequently does not succeed. It is too simple, not totally understood, and too easy for them to refuse.

Time must be spent with the students involved in an honest discussion and study of the perilous activity. They must be educated in such a way that *they*, themselves, come to totally recognize and understand the existing dangers involved in the risky behaviors. *They* must see the high risk, understand it, and willingly repudiate its engagement themselves.

Most youngsters remain optimistic in relation to events taking place in their lives—and that's OK—usually. There are, however, certain appealing activities that pose a steady, genuine danger to their well-being—smoking, substance abuse, becoming sexually active at an early age, violence, unhealthy diet, and so on.

Now, their optimism gives many eager adolescents an active, positive attitude toward life. Though this may afford them an enjoyable existence much of the time, it may also diminish their perception of danger, reduce common sense, and promote denial. It then becomes the responsibility of the older generation to clarify and intensify their abilities to recognize the existence of these threats.

The teacher, however, cannot simply blurt out, "Don't do it!" In order to convince this younger age group, students need to be moved *unconventionally, respectfully, educationally, emotionally, and slowly—in steps, rising level by level and beginning at a point parallel to their present position and mind-set.* (Need to read that again? Go ahead.)

The approach:

The following suggested method can be used in regard to many perilous behaviors. For the purpose of offering an example, please look at the dangers of *smoking*. Though you may not be a health teacher, this approach can still offer you a realistic look at the typical adolescent mind and ways to successfully deal with it.

The class could be instructed to jot down on a piece of paper the main reason they believe some young people begin smoking. (The top response would more than likely be "It's cool" or "It looks cool.")

Follow this piece with the question "How many of you honestly think that it does look cool?" (*Begin at a point parallel to their present position and mind-set.*)

Respond by accepting their reasoning. To them, it *does* look cool (or whatever the top response happens to be). Write it down on a board at the front of the room. In doing so, you are not agreeing with them; you are, however, declaring that you understand their reasoning and allowing them to have a voice, even if the reasoning is unrealistic. Consequently, you are placing yourself in a friendlier, accepting position: "I understand why you feel this way."

Next question: "Why are so many adults in opposition to teenage smoking?"

In this segment, their responses will likely offer health dangers that they've frequently heard but, quite possibly, not seriously considered as likely to affect *them*. Let them discuss these responses and receive a closer, more realistic view of the danger.

Now it is time to leave the room—not physically, just mentally and educationally.

The next step could be to view the most informative and relevant video that you can find. It should realistically and sensibly explain why the decision to begin inhaling cigarette smoke is incredibly perilous and senseless. This could be a video that realistically displays actual views of affected human lungs, destroyed cilia, cancer tumors, hospital patients with gravelly voices, and so on. The individuals in the presentation need to be authentic, medical professionals or individuals physically affected by smoke inhalations—not actors. Use significant information and irrefutable proof.

More discussion should follow the video, with no lecturing by the teacher. Allow class members to offer comments based on the video's information. "Does anyone in the room know someone who has suffered in similar ways? It is not necessary to mention names." Keep the discussion going. "Does that person still smoke? Did she attempt to quit? Why do you think she didn't succeed?"

In the next class session, perhaps offer transparencies, photographs, quotes from doctors, or any kind of overwhelming documented evidence. Let these be fodder for more discussion.

Following that, it is time for firsthand testimonies from those affected by cigarette smoking: former smokers; witnesses; nurses; retired doctors; radiologists; X-ray technicians; or a letter, e-mail, or phone call from the Mayo Clinic, National Institutes of Health, county health center, Centers for Disease Control, and so on. Invite one or two nearby professionals to your classroom to offer a presentation. Class members will have been inundated with indisputable, clear evidence. The majority will find it very difficult to refute the *no-smoking message*. Let more discussion follow these presentations.

Next, introduce factual information not yet discussed: "The Centers for Disease Control recently announced that the average smoker loses eleven years of life because of smoking. However, that's only an average. I'm sure that some smokers lose only four or five years of living rather than eleven." Pause for clarity. Four or five *years*. "Four or five years, four or five birthdays, four or five Christmases." Pause. "Then again, if eleven is the *average*, then I suppose some lose nineteen or twenty years of life." Write this on a board at the front of the room. Large numbers: "19–20 *years*."

Move to another part of the board and, in order to truly underscore the serious reality of your message, begin writing the months of the year. When you reach June, quietly enlist the help of several students to join you by creating their own list of months visible to all. Let it go on for a while, until six, nine, or more yearly lists of months are displayed. You more than likely will not have room for nineteen lists of the twelve months in a year. This is a message in itself. Take the time; have the class join together in reading the months aloud. Ask for their thoughts.

Long pause. Discussion.

This will take several days, of course. However, by the time you reach this stage in your lessons, their judgment may very well have moved more closely parallel to your point of view.

Regardless of the topic—smoking, unhealthy diet, substance abuse, violent behavior, human sexuality, prejudice (worth repeating)—the teacher stands a much stronger chance of succeeding if she moves unconventionally, respectfully, educationally, emotionally, slowly—in steps, rising level by level, beginning at a point parallel to the students' present position and mind-set.

Following this type of step-by-step, non-lecturing method, your students have a better chance of selecting a wiser direction in making life choices. They are not *instructed* as to what to do; they are encouraged to respectfully make *their own decisions* after overwhelming, persuasive evidence is introduced to them in a fair, unintimidating manner. Sufficient time is given for thought and discussion. Evidence is offered thoroughly and clearly from excellent sources. They are treated respectfully, sincerely, as though you care—and, of course, you do.

Encourage honest responses during a discussion. After several class members voluntarily share their decisions not to smoke (and this will occur), it is time for *your* clear and honest opinion stated slowly, dramatically, and sensibly explaining, perhaps, how and when you made the same decision as they. The more emotional the revelation, the greater its effect and the more easily they may come to identify with it.

LEARNING FROM EXPERIENCE NO. 14: THE TEACHERS' CONFERENCE

You've attended a conference with several colleagues. There were a number of speakers, and the majority of the information was rather new, unique, and considered useful. As the day continued, you compared your notes with your colleagues' and, during lunch, jotted down some helpful material that you missed. On the way home, the group of you discussed the enlightening knowledge and agreed that the experience was worth the trip. Is that it? The experience is completed?

No. Now you must spend energy within a very brief time span planning how to utilize the new skills and information. Do not "put it on hold"! You've heard the expression, "Use it or lose it"? The longer you wait, the less likely you will be to introduce it to your classes. Review the information with your colleagues. Perhaps discuss with them your classes' responses to the material's introduction. Keep the dialogue going. You say you already knew this? Fine. Simply treat this message as a reminder.

LEARNING FROM EXPERIENCE NO. 15: TOUCHING

Some of them move right in: one hand on the top of your desk and the other hand on your shoulder. They need it? They like it? They're used to it?

Does touching give them a feeling of bonding, affection, attention? If it is an appropriate kind of touching and you still have the individual's educational attention, why can't it continue? Are you all right with it? Might you have to adjust to it? Were you ready? Did you know it would occur? Following your introduction to it, adjustment to it, and understanding of it, why not simply apply it? Touch them! In fun, in support, in making better contact, in allowing them to know that you like them and *care*.

Keep in mind: The kids who offer the impression that they don't wish to be touched frequently are the ones who *need* it and may ultimately *respond* to it in a positive manner.

LEARNING FROM EXPERIENCE NO. 16: BECOMING HUMAN

Arrange one or two family photos on your desk. When students see them, it may be easier for them to picture you in a lifestyle familiar to them. "My teacher is married!" "My teacher is a mom." Rather than being seen as the person who enters a classroom environment, dressed appropriately, distributing papers, assignments, directions, and commands, you begin to come across as being more human—more like a mom or dad or even more like themselves—human!

After they've seen your family photos, you may find them staring at you for periods of time. Good! Could be a sign of understanding, acceptance, or even fondness.

NOTE

1. Misbehavior is not restricted only to boys; girls may participate, as well. Each of the examples, however, will often abstain from using both male and female pronouns simply for reasons of reading simplicity.

Part III

TOOLS THAT SUCCEED
Unconventional Approaches and Strategies

Chapter Four

Unique and Unorthodox Approaches in Education

From time to time, you'll notice the use of the term *unorthodox* being used in content. The intended definition of the word would be "unconventional," "untraditional," "thought-provoking," "unexpected," or even "inspiring." Using common, expected, conventional methods in one's teaching can succeed with many students. But these methods are not likely to consistently produce substantial curiosity, attention, or progress with *all* students.

The following two chapters present several useful approaches categorized as different or unorthodox. Numerous other unconventional activities can be found in chapters 6 and 7. Your students may easily find them thought-provoking, motivating, even fascinating. Try something different—something they'll find inspiring.

Unorthodox classroom strategies, when engaged by most educators, serve to help in obtaining student involvement, attention, amusement, and appreciation. Treat them like kids. Approach them from *their* direction. Think as they do. This helps obtain their complete attention in an alternative manner that would be truly motivating.

These tactics quickly gather their attention, inspire their thought processes, and get your point across in the most potentially successful manner. Being different may also persuade these young people to take a closer look at their teacher—and thus you may come off as unusual, cool, strange, or even weird but worthy of watching as a teacher to whom they listen. These kids can easily tell when the teacher sees the world through their eyes, understands, and accepts them for who they are. Your classroom can be unique, atypical. Students will, thus, be drawn into your lesson by instinct and interest. What could be better?

On the first day of school, for example, why not confront the obvious? Following your fire drill instructions, classroom rules and expectations, discussion of materials, scheduling questions, and so on, why not offer something like this: "I've always felt that it's kind of tough giving up summer. I can still remember leaving my home on my first day of school, saying good-bye to my dog and heading up the road, carrying all my school supplies while thinking, 'I hope today goes OK.' Did anyone have any particular thoughts or feelings today? What's the change from summer vacation to the first day of school like for you?"

There may be interest in pursuing the topic "The First Day of School" (or something similar) for a bit. If that's the case, fine. Encourage responses. Get them talking. Try not to be critical of what you hear. Capture their attention, and gently *reel them in*. They will begin to relax a bit during the discussion; they'll also begin to know the teacher better. Nearly any type of friendly discussion would be fine.

Then, after a bit of time, while engaging all the eyes in the room, perhaps offer something like, "I think you're going to like it here. I can't wait to get started. I will do my best to present an interesting course and not bore you. So, uh, please try not to bore *me*." Allow them the opportunity to get used to your voice, your manner, your enthusiasm for teaching. The instructor must assure them that they are safe, among friends, and things will be fine. However, they *will* be educationally challenged.

During the dialogue, walk the room; don't simply occupy the *teacher's arena*, delivering first-day information. Move closer; allow heads to turn. Encourage it. Get closer to them. Read their eyes; let them read yours. Offer a sincere, receptive expression, and maintain your very best attention. If you're able to retain their eye contact, the students will usually experience difficulty hiding the truth from you. You can, then, summon your perceptive ability and have it go to work for you. Who are they really? What's going on in their minds? Get to know your students.

On the next day of school, begin developing a positive classroom atmosphere by taking the first step in creating a *team* of students. Help them in acquiring better cooperative and team-building skills along with building trust and developing the courage to stand out in taking positive risks—a willingness to *try*. (Suggestions as to how to go about developing the team approach begin with chapter 6. Please look it over.)

It isn't likely that any group of students on their own could focus, work as a team, and effectively promote bonding and cooperation. A teacher's yearly plan should be to address this educational necessity at one's first opportunity. Additionally, subtly assure the kids that your classroom could possibly be considerably different from the majority of experiences they'd already had.

In going along with the idea of unconventional approaches, please consider the following.

"IT ISN'T FAIR"

You've heard the words "It's not fair!" or "School's not fair!" Some teachers may be tempted to respond, "Well, life's not fair."

Really? Life isn't fair to us? Might the adolescent thereafter entertain the notion "What did I do to deserve an unfair life?" or "Then why try?" Think about it; is the response at all helpful? How about addressing the cause of the outburst or encouraging a short discussion instead of just whisking away the student's emotional complaint with an impractical statement?

Or, consider an additional possibility: Following the complaint(s), suggest a discussion (taking place immediately or planned for a later time) based on what some see as the unfairness of school. When the opportunity for discussion arrives, engage the topic by asking everyone to respond to a request: "Write down two things that are unfair about school." Allow sufficient time.

Explain that difficulties within the school environment are like all difficulties; the individual experiencing the problem is not always able to perceive a quick solution, but help is available. One needs to find it. Then, pair off into groups of two for a conversation based on ways school is perceived as unfair.

Allow each student to voice a complaint concerning the unfairness of school. Then, offer the partners an opportunity to help. What can be done about the complaints? Explain that you'd like to give each student an opportunity to suggest a remedy in helping the classmate deal with what is seen as difficult or *unfair*. The technique used in this lesson is to write "prescriptions" for the difficulties.

Generally speaking, *prescriptions* are what doctors give patients to make them *feel better*. Likewise, this activity gives everyone an opportunity to recommend a "remedy" for a variety of different concerns in order to help a classmate *feel better*. We must keep in mind that some complaints will not be resolved by a conversation with one other individual. Therefore, this activity can be followed by repeating it in groups of four or within an open class discussion.

When the problems and complaints are shared with the entire class, students can think about *prescriptions* and write them down on paper. One option might be to have the proposed solutions remain anonymous. The approach on the part of a student offering a prescription could begin, "For those of you not having enough time to visit lockers between classes, I suggest the following . . ."

All *prescriptions* could be placed in a container and read aloud by individuals over the course of a day or two (devoting short periods of time) for all to hear, or they could be delivered directly to the individual in need. If anyone wishes to report back to the class on engaging the "remedy," then this would be an appropriate possibility.[3]

When students complain that school isn't fair, pause for a moment, then honestly respond,

> I think you're right. You walk into a classroom, sit in a hard chair, and can't get up to walk around. You have to listen to some man or woman talk about what he or she thinks is important for forty-three minutes. You then have three minutes to get to another room, where it starts all over again.
>
> You are sometimes forced to study a subject that doesn't appeal to you and have to take work home when you leave the school. Yeah, I agree, in a strong way, it just doesn't sound fair.
>
> But, you know what? Presently, *it's the best we have to offer!* I would love to be able to change some things to make the whole day more appealing. By gosh, I'd get bean bags for everybody, change the fluorescent lights to softer illumination, add wall-to-wall carpeting in every classroom, put in a swimming pool and an outdoor ropes course. Then, I'd arrange a hike or dance every month. Yeah, that's what I'd do. I, however, do not have the authority, so here's what *I* say:
>
> Do whatever the heck you need to do to make it through your classes. Tell your younger brother not to come into your bedroom when you're doing your homework, go for hikes on weekends with pals, treat yourself

to the best novels and movies you can find, get plenty of sleep, tell terrific jokes to your friends, laugh until you fall on the floor, cry when you're sad, volunteer at a dog kennel and maybe take home a black lab. Just do it—whatever you have to do—put in six years of your best work! *Do it!* (Delivered, perhaps, with considerable volume.)

After a pause, with a softer tone:

Then, not that long from now, when your name is called, walk across the stage wearing your cap and gown and accept your diploma. Following that, go to as many graduation parties as you can. Then *leave town!*

When you're eighteen or nineteen, leaving town won't seem quite as intimidating as it may appear right now. Further your education; pursue your dream. In time, maybe even get married after a few years. Want to move back here? Terrific, I'll be glad to see you. Bring your degree with you. You'll be making more money than I am, but that's OK; I'll still like you. *Just do it!* (Oh, yeah—once again, raise your voice a bit to really capture their attention; it drives it home more strongly and shows them how intensely you believe in it.)

This might also be a good time to pursue a second step to the experience: "Write down two things that you *like* about school." Take the same approach you did earlier. Perhaps some kids are overlooking some of the pleasant, more positive things about the school setting. If they think about it, they *will* come up with a list. And, if no one mentions how important these kids are to their teachers and school personnel who work with them, remind them—enthusiastically!

Some of the complaints vocalized during the last activity may, more than likely, be concerns about homework. The following approach can be unquestionably helpful to you and your students.

RECIPE FOR HOMEWORK SUCCESS

The following activity includes all lesson details used in its development. The reader is asked to initially read it in its entirety. If, at a later time, you wish to engage the shorter, formatted "lesson plan" version, it exists within the appendix, lesson 1.

Because concerns and complaints about homework are frequently exchanged among class members, the following task might help the class find productive solutions to their problems:

- Initiate a discussion about homework, allowing your pupils to talk about the daily responsibilities in any manner they wish—even venting. Then, divide students into groups of two, directing them to focus on complaints expressed by classmates earlier in the lesson and to discuss ways of addressing the concerns in a positive fashion. (Each student may take brief notes.)
- After bringing the group back together in a total class community meeting (described later), ask that they brainstorm solutions to one concern at a time as you write them clearly on a SMART Board, newsprint, or elsewhere.

Following that, propose that the suggestions be included in a "Recipe for Homework Success" (a list of strategies to be considered by classmates). How can they help each other succeed?

Write each item on the board, newsprint, or screen at the front of the room, and discuss it thoroughly. When the class is satisfied with the coverage and the possible benefit of the suggestions, print them clearly and neatly. Display the list. Additionally, copy the information on individual sheets to be passed out among the kids.

The following is a list of typical suggestions offered by numerous students:

- Don't forget to use your assignment pad or iPad for documenting homework assignments.
- Be sure that you understand the directions before leaving school.
- Make good use of study halls.
- Organize your materials in your binder and in your locker.
- Do your work at the same time daily (early), and follow a schedule.
- Find a quiet, comfortable place to work away from the TV.
- Don't procrastinate.
- Take a break if you have a lot to do.
- Put completed homework in a place where you won't lose or forget it.[2]

Perhaps conclude by asking class members to write down ways in which they may benefit through the use of the suggestions on the list. In class, refer to the list when necessary, or add to it.

EARLY-BIRD SPECIAL

A useful strategy in persuading students to be time conscious: On days when planning to give a pop quiz, place a bonus question, along with its answer, on the board right beneath a map or large sheet of paper that can be rolled up or down. At precisely thirty seconds before the bell begins the period, pull the map or sheet of paper down to conceal the bonus question. Anyone arriving after that time misses the opportunity to obtain the bonus points. This encourages students to get to class as early as possible on a regular basis, especially because they do not know in advance when there is a pop quiz.

Chapter Five

Are You Listening to Your Students?

Do you enjoy teaching? You do? Great! It would then follow that you enjoy kids. That is fortunate—because occasions will more than likely occur when you'll find yourself in a position of impending responsibility as you're approached by a student in need. In need of what? In need of *you*! This is the kid (boy or girl) who is looking for understanding, advice, attention, possibly even safety—and, most importantly, someone to *listen* to her. And somewhere along the line, she got the notion that you could supply what is missing in her life at that particular time.

For those of you with years of experience, this has more than likely already occurred. Individuals new to the profession, prepare for this; it *will* occur. Included in this chapter are some responses and techniques that you could employ on those occasions when you're:

- driving into the parking lot a bit early,
- sitting at your desk at 3:45 correcting papers, or perhaps
- saying good night to the school secretary

and are approached by a student requesting your attention and help. (Easily perceived; it's in the facial expression, especially, of course, the eyes.)

First of all, when it becomes obvious that she wishes to talk to you, be certain that enough time is available. If not, briefly explain to her that you are absolutely interested in carrying on the conversation. However, for her benefit, you need an occasion where you'll not be required to deal with interruptions as well as having enough time and space to be at your best. So, if necessary, arrange an appointment. Stress the importance of the meeting and how *strongly* you wish to engage in the discussion.

Then, when the time is right and the student begins to explain the problem, please consider keeping responses in mind similar to these:

- Make solid eye contact and lean into the conversation.
- Be accepting, even if you initially disagree with something she says.
- As she is speaking, use *cultural fillers* from time to time ("Is that right?" "I understand." "Really!" "Uh-huh."). In this way, the speaker knows you are listening intently.
- Encourage more communication: "Tell me more." "Would you like to talk about it?" "How did you feel about that?" "Then what happened?"

Use *reflective listening*: Feed back to the speaker words that disclose how you perceive her; listen to the feelings behind the speaker's remarks.

Sometimes, *you* end up informing the *youngster* how she feels. "Sounds like he made you pretty angry." "You seem really sad." "You sound anxious about this concern." "I'll bet that's very frustrating to you." "You really get angry when he says that, don't you?"

The most *powerful* inquiry (when offered at precisely the right time): After you notice a student's facial expression move toward an even darker sadness, or when a break occurs in her voice, or possibly a long pause, you then can ask the most influential question (slowly and softly): *"How are you feeling right now?"* Pause.

What is the number 1 response from a kid who has reached this point in relating a sorrowful experience? Yes, you're right: *tears*. I believe that there's nothing wrong with this. You know what they say about a "good cry." When it's time to cry, we should cry; when it's time to laugh, we laugh. Laughing and crying balance our emotions, our lives. Additionally, it may prompt the student to offer even more information about the event than she prepared to or, in some cases, was even *aware of*. Be patient and perhaps place a supportive hand on her shoulder.

Paraphrase: Let the speaker know that you've heard her by repeating it in your own words:

"So, you're feeling quite lonely right now because she told you she would call to discuss the dance coming up this weekend and didn't. Am I correct?"

Summarize: Highlight the main points.

"Here's what I hear you saying . . ."
"If I understand you correctly, you're saying that . . ."

Condense it.

Barriers to communication may occur when the teacher is responding only to the facts rather than the speaker's feelings:

- Do not offer quick solutions: Quick-fix remedies may give the student the impression that you think she is not smart enough to figure it out alone.
- Avoid making quick judgments: "You're taking this too seriously." "I'd just stop talking to that person if I were you." This does not help.
- Do not minimize the problem: "I'm sure you'll feel differently about this in a week or so." Again, it is not the solution to the existing problem for the kid.
- Don't take the floor away from the speaker by interjecting your experience concerning a similar problem: "The same thing happened to me; here's what I did."[4]

During this conversation, you are justifying her feelings, her reaction to the event, and even any confusion she is possibly experiencing. Additionally, remember, you are fulfilling her number 1 need—someone who will listen intently without interrupting. That's right; the number 1 need: someone who will listen—just *listen*.

Be prepared; you may find time flying by, but think of what you are doing for this student. This may be exactly what is needed. Will she feel better? More than likely. Will she remember? What do you think? And what about her self-confidence? Yes, frequently stronger. You were there for her; that means a great deal to these kids.

Now, I'm not suggesting that you can do the same kind of work that a clinical psychologist does. You must be careful in knowing when to suggest a visit to the school psychologist or guidance counselor. However, if the student approaches you, what else should you do at that particular time other than be of help?

Some educators may not see it as part of their job. They may wish to accept no part of the responsibility. If this is their desire, then so be it. In that case, perhaps a referral can promptly be made to another qualified professional.

Chapter Six

Cooperative Classroom Environment

Here are four team-building activities that can promote communication as well as positive attitudes among your students, enabling them to work together more effectively within a *cooperative environment*.

TEAMBUILDING ACTIVITIES

Activity 1: The Milling Assassin
Activity 2: Encouraging Positive Communication
Activity 3: Developing the Classroom Contract
Activity 4: Seat of Distinction (see chapter 7)

Activities 1, 2, and 3 were created by Dr. Gerald Edwards, Phil Olynciw, and their colleagues, associated with the Northeast Regional Center for Drug-Free Schools and Communities. Dr. Edwards was chairman of the Health Education Department of Adelphi University in Garden City, New York, and director of the Adelphi University National Training Institute, sponsored by the US Office of Education. Their curriculum and activities are referred to as "Project Team."

Before moving directly into the *team building activities*, it would be beneficial for the reader to become familiar with one of Gerry and Phil's exceedingly successful creations: the *community meeting*. This technique is extremely helpful, not only as the setting for the activities contained in this chapter, but also within any lesson designed to have students totally absorb a topic while feeling connected, supported, and actively involved. This class session, designed and promoted by these men, works smoothly

The Community Meeting

This is a setting within which students are free to pursue a relevant topic, asking and answering questions along with stating opinions related to the issue. Consequently, they can review, debate, and progress with a better understanding of the subject in a timely fashion. This activity increases better *community interaction* and helps to build a positive support system among participants.

As opinions are generated, the teacher may record the views in the front of the room for all to see. One of the rules is, *No raising of hands*. Once the format is understood, experienced, and accepted, students work effectively and efficiently within the environment. The list of student suggestions or questions will begin to develop within a very brief period of time.

Rationale

The lesson provides:

- feedback from students on a recently learned subject or a relevant topic being discussed and
- a forum within which questions and opinions may be generated and information within a particular subject clarified.

It allows for:

- reinforcement of learning,
- building support and confidence among participants,
- a sharing of positive and negative feelings,
- a large amount of interaction among participants, and
- exploration of further issues.

Rules

- Stay on task; keep to the *here and now*.
- Only one person speaks at a time.

- No hand raising.
- Share thoughts with the entire group, not the individual sitting next to you.
- When speaking, use the pronoun *I*, speaking only for yourself, rather than the collective *we*.
- On occasion, the teacher may address a student asking for an opinion.

This approach unlocks the door to *open dialogue* among students. Everyone is free to offer views and suggestions regarding a particular topic. A setting then begins to develop within which class members enjoy spontaneous, uninhibited feedback. Issues and topics can thus be discussed to a point where a greater interest and understanding is acquired by students *as well as the teacher*. Participants cannot help but to employ more effective listening skills as the discussion moves forward.

As progress is made, the energy level remains high, with the kids totally focused on the subject being discussed. Students, while feeling vigorously engaged and supported, more easily comprehend topics being pursued. And finally, a positive support system begins to emerge among participants. If comments offered become difficult to hear or understand, then the teacher can bring this to the attention of the students.

Gerry Edwards and Phil Olynciw called the next two activities—"The Milling Assassin" and "Developing the Classroom Contract"—*humanizing* sessions. The approaches help to develop an atmosphere of friendly exchange. A classroom teacher needs students to participate, cooperate, and work as a team. The following activities help create just that: an environment of positive relationships that serve to enhance teamwork and then learning. Three of the *humanizing* sessions are described in the following paragraphs and one in chapter 7.

ACTIVITY 1: THE MILLING ASSASSIN[5]

The following activity includes all lesson details used in its development. The reader is asked to initially read it in its entirety. If, at a later time, you wish to engage the shorter, formatted "lesson plan" version, it exists within the appendix, lesson 2.

"The Milling Assassin" is an introductory activity. It functions as a *first step* in the process of peer acceptance, bonding, and team building. Though it may sound rather strange at first, it has benefits not immediately perceived. One may initially feel uncertain of its potential until tested out; results will be totally positive. It works. Try it.

interacting + bonding = better communication

"The Milling Assassin" is used as an energizer for the kids, an ice-breaker. It opens the door to the humanizing phenomenon, helping participants see classmates in a different light while encouraging the kids to interact with each other through unique and unconventional interactions. Furthermore, it helps build trust among class members. It is the type of endeavor that they, most likely, never experienced in any classroom situation.

Participants move about, totally involved, chuckling, even touching. While engaged in this activity, they begin to view their peers (and ultimately their teacher) as who they truly are. If you happen to view any uncomfortable behavior, then you may wish to capitalize on it by later discussing why those feelings were understandably experienced. The individuals displaying those particular behaviors should remain anonymous.

Introduction

This activity may be presented to groups ranging in age from early adolescence to adult.

Procedure

The two strategies suggested here are helpful in *setting the stage*—getting the group in an appropriate frame of mind. However, if you are experiencing time restraints, one or both can be eliminated if necessary.

Introduce the following: What are two strategies that help us in dealing with personal problems, discomfort, and disappointment? (Then display the answers.)

Written on a board in the front of the room: *A support network* and *A sense of humor.*

A. *A support network:* Friends and family members available to be approached with personal concerns. "When you are experiencing any kind of difficulties—school problems, personal problems, health concerns, and so on—and feel a need for support and advice, what steps can you take?"

"You can seek help from trusted friends and family. This is essential for everyone. We all need this type of assistance at times in our lives."
- Without disclosing names, each student is encouraged to have one or more friends or family members in mind during this part of the lesson.
- Briefly discuss examples of support experienced by the teacher and class members along with the advantages of utilizing the assistance.

B. *A sense of humor:* Humor can help *reframe* potentially depressing situations, promote the release of endorphins, and assist in building resilience within an individual. A well-functioning sense of humor helps one to see difficult conditions in a different, more realistic manner. One can laugh at a situation more easily and respond to life's struggles more effectively with humor rather than anger.
- Offer amusing occurrences from your life that helped you deal with challenging times from your past.
- Ask for humorous examples from the class. Brief discussion. Then, taking advantage of their amused frames of mind, move immediately from the existing humorous environment into the following activity.

Introduce "The Milling Assassin," explaining the rules and procedure beforehand. Members of the class stand and form a circle, eyes closed, hands behind their backs. The facilitator moves around the outside of the circle, pulling on the index finger of each participant—all except for the student secretly chosen by the facilitator to portray the "Milling Assassin." His or her finger is ignored. Instead, the middle of the palm is touched. (The individual is not forewarned.) With that, the teacher announces, "Go ahead and mill." Kids can be reminded that it is a nonverbal activity (no talking at all).

They wander about the front of the room, shaking hands with classmates. If they giggle a bit, that is helpful in breaking the ice, the barriers.

Whenever the assassin feels he or she can get away with it, along with shaking the hand, the index finger is extended to touch the wrist area of the unsuspecting classmate.

With that, the individual receiving the *death tap* (as the teacher earlier instructed) silently counts to ten, then falls to the floor, making any appropriate vocal noises he or she may wish. No one else may, at that time, say a word about who is suspected as the assassin. Counting to ten allows the assassin to move away from the *victim* and not be easily identified.

If a student feels that he or she knows who the assassin is, a hand may be raised, and the facilitator stops the action. The teacher may then ask the class for a second individual to raise a hand in order to *back up* the guess yet to be made by the first individual. (You need two participants involved to officially offer a guess as to the identity of the assassin.)

After someone volunteers to *back up* the first student, he or she is then given the opportunity to identify the assassin. If the individuals are correct, then the assassin has been successfully identified, and the first session concludes. If the individuals are incorrect, both also die and fall to the floor.

Continue milling until the *culprit* is identified.

This activity gives students opportunities to see different characteristics of their classmates' personalities. It helps by bringing to the surface personal traits that are not frequently visible within a classroom environment. By discovering other dimensions of their classmates' personalities, they get to know one another better, feel more strongly connected, and become more accepting.

The ice has been broken.[5]

Processing the Activity

Processing is a procedure that offers a *look back*; a manner of reviewing an activity in such a way that the participants better understand its purpose as well as examine what they were thinking and doing during the flow. They may then more easily perceive the benefits of engaging the lesson and what can be learned from it.

Processing could include the use of helpful questions, such as:

- Why do you think I introduced the lesson?
- What did you learn?

- What surprised you?
- What kind of classmate would really enjoy this activity?
- What would you change in the activity to make the lesson better?
- How are you feeling about what we just did?

The processing component may include feedback from the teacher describing what he or she had observed (no names need be mentioned). Observations might include the speed with which the activity was initiated; the types of conversations exchanged; how many got out of their chairs first or last; how many approached a classmate quickly, slowly, quietly, enthusiastically; how many smiled; and so on.

This approach allows the class an opportunity to understand the participants' different interpretations of the task. It can encourage more enthusiastic behavior on the part of some kids in future lessons, regardless of the type of activities engaged.

Example of a teacher's processing: "I observed several rise from their chairs rather quickly and begin searching for a classmate with whom to shake hands. The majority of the class, however, rose more slowly, heads turning to look around the room, and did not seem to be in a hurry. This appears rather normal for a group this size. I've seen the same reaction with seventh-graders, high school seniors, teachers, and parents. Now I could be wrong, but some seemed, well, a bit reluctant at first, to get moving but then eventually joined in. Why do you suppose some moved in this fashion?"

During the discussion, a class member may offer something similar to the following: "They were uncertain/hesitant/looked a bit uncomfortable in becoming involved." Participants are then free to conclude that this *uncertainty* is common and normal—and thus, if they hesitated to become immediately involved, they should not be concerned; it's typical. Consequently, with greater confidence during the next activity (whatever that may be), they'll not likely hold back as much. Perhaps, conclude with the message "The truth is, I enjoyed every moment!"

Processing helps everyone understand how the class is doing and validates the reality that some class members have different perceptions and reactions to the task (as well as to life itself). They might, therefore, come to recognize that their classmates may be viewing the lesson in a different manner. Consequently, this perception may possibly give them a new perspective on the activity as well as on their peers. Additionally, some may respond to future encounters with greater eagerness and optimism.

Repeat the activity if is there is time and interest.[6]

If your response to this activity is "You gotta be kidding!" that is understandable, but hold on. As indicated earlier, unorthodox approaches have a greater tendency to be successful rather than unsuccessful. Additionally, the "Milling Assassin" is almost unanimously accepted by participants of all ages. Catch them a bit off guard; employ totally unsuspected types of engagements; show them that your approach is distinctive and applied with them in mind. Unsure? Perhaps return to the introduction of this section and read again the activity's purpose. Then decide.

ACTIVITY 2: ENCOURAGING POSITIVE COMMUNICATION

A. Introduction to Successful Listening

The following activity includes all lesson details used in its development. The reader is asked to initially read it in its entirety. If, at a later time, you wish to engage the shorter, formatted "lesson plan" version, it exists within the appendix, lesson 3a.

At this point, it would be advantageous to revisit a topic described earlier in chapter 5, "Are You Listening to Your Students?" This is a lesson devoted to skills used when successfully listening to one's students. This time, it's the kids' turn to listen to each other.

Begin with some or all of the following questions on a screen, a board, or newsprint:

- How well do members of our society listen to each other?
- How do you know when an individual is listening to you? (One can judge by behavior, body language, facial expressions, etc.)
- How do you know when an individual is *not* listening to you?
- How does one feel when a person is listening to his or her words?
- How does one feel when a person is not listening to his or her words?

- Why is it sometimes difficult to listen? What does it mean to *actively* listen?
- Why is listening important?

Stop listening!

As a method of truly emphasizing the importance of listening, ask a student to speak to you about an important topic. Encourage the participant to choose a topic that is recent, significant, and known to everyone in the room. Role-play the *nonlistener*, the individual who makes minimal efforts, sounds, and gestures in an effort to persuade the speaker to believe that he or she is listening.

When the speaker begins engaging the topic, behave in the following manner: eyes move quickly from side to side, head turns, glance at your wristwatch or the wall clock, continually nod, shuffle papers on your desk, repeat "Yep, yep" with little if any real eye contact.

Following the verbal attempt, ask the speaker how he or she feels about your reaction. ("Left out, unimportant, unsuccessful, like you didn't care about me or what I had to say.") Then ask the individual to engage in delivering the message again. This time hold still, lean forward, maintain eye contact, nod from time to time, and use verbal "cultural fillers" ("I see." "Really!" "Hard to believe!" "No kidding!"), as well as facial responses. Once again, ask how the speaker feels. It is not difficult to anticipate the dissimilar reaction. Emphasize the importance of listening; we all need to do it. Can we all improve? *Yes!*

B. A Listening Activity

At this point, the teacher may introduce the skills to employ when practicing the art of successful listening. Techniques and approaches are discussed in chapter 5. (Not only can a teacher benefit from utilizing the procedure, but students may gain, as well.)

Skills to be covered:

- Reflective Listening
- Summarizing

- Paraphrasing
- Avoiding Barriers to Communication

(Definitions and methods of usage are available in chapter 5.)

After covering these skills, instruct the class to develop a two- or three-minute message to verbally share with a classmate. The message could be based on almost anything—opinions, events, sports, future plans in life. Then, explain the following strategies (listener and speaker responsibilities) while demonstrating how to engage them. Students should, of course, be given sufficient time to study the task in preparation.

Divide the kids into groups of two, a speaker and a listener. Following three- to five-minute engagements, instruct each of the two to feed back to the other thoughts, feelings, and observations concerning the exchange along with what was heard. What transpired? How did it succeed? Following that, reverse the roles. Additionally, if time, have a duo go through the activity in the center of the room. Then, review the experience using comments from the entire class (Fig. 6.1).[7]

Processing the listening activity can also help to promote a better understanding of time spent. This is the same approach used earlier in this chapter:

- Why do you think I introduced the lesson?
- What did you learn?
- What surprised you?
- What kind of student would really like this activity?
- What would you change in the activity to make the lesson better?
- How are you feeling about what we just did?

Conclude by describing any significant behaviors you observed.

C. The Next Step: What Stops Some Students from Becoming Enthusiastically Engaged in a Class Activity?

The following activity includes all lesson details used in its development. The reader is asked to initially read it in its entirety. If, at a later time, you wish to engage the shorter, formatted "lesson plan" version, it exists within the appendix, lesson 3b.

Listener

Focusing	*Attending*	*Reaction*
-Finds a purpose for listening	-Decides whether message is organized	-Asks for further clarification
-Is prepared to deal with major distractions	-Tries to anticipate speaker's point(s)	-Feeds back major points
	-Accepts or rejects them	
-Is ready and willing to be attentive	-Asks for clarification	-Voices concerns constructively
-Attempts to be open-minded	-Evaluates	
	-Remains sensitive to non-verbal messages	

Speaker

Focusing	*Attending*	*Reaction*
-Prepares message with a purpose	-Presents message in a clear and organized manner	-Accepts and responds to questions
-Decides what to say and how to say it	-Speaks clearly with appropriate volume and speed	-Is sensitive to listener's reaction
-Feels free to use non-verbal communication	-Is open to constructive criticism	

Figure 6.1

Where do we go from here? Engage in a lesson where the pupils discuss common difficulties that occur when an individual is simply not working up to his or her potential. On occasions, we've all noticed when certain kids are reluctant to participate in class activities. Can these problems be addressed?

Without question! Additionally, the students will see evidence of the teacher's fairness, patience, understanding, and *respect*.

Positive communication, Active listening, Working up to potential

All function together in increasing academic success.

Introduce and pursue the following topics. During the student interaction, walk the room, observing examples of students' use of the listening skills.

1. "What is it about *others* that stops me from becoming enthusiastically engaged in a class activity?"

- Individual responses on paper. Grammar and spelling do *not* apply.
- Discussion with a partner. Share, discuss, and make suggestions.
- Time permitting: Discussion in groups of four. Share, discuss, and make suggestions.
- Class discussion in a community meeting.
- Instruct participants to silently write *prescriptions* (see chapter 4), making suggestions to help deal with the concerns shared earlier by classmates.
- The teacher or a student reads the responses, or the teacher hands them out to appropriate students in need of suggestive help. Further discussions would be at the discretion of the teacher and class.

Rationale

It gives students an opportunity to:

- see evidence of others' frustration ("I'm not the only one.");
- relieve some of *their* frustration;
- discover solutions to some of their problems; and
- see evidence of teacher's fairness, patience, understanding, and respect.

2. "What is it about *me* that stops me from becoming enthusiastically engaged in a class activity?"

Follow the same process: individual responses, discussions with partners, groups of four, community meeting, prescriptions.

It is important for students to understand why, on occasion, they may not *feel like* becoming involved in small- or large-group activities. Their reluctance is sometimes caused by those with whom they work, while at other times it may be caused by their own views and moods. Are they aware of this? Possibly not. In either case, steps can be taken to better understand and counteract the problem.

Processing this activity could be quite helpful. Is the problem always caused by the kids?

Is it sometimes caused by the school environment, professionals, schedules, educational demands? Without question! One successful way of gaining better support from students is by giving them a measure of involvement in designing the academic environment and routine of daily lessons. Consider the following activity.

ACTIVITY 3: DEVELOPING THE CLASSROOM CONTRACT

The following activity includes all lesson details used in its development. The reader is asked to initially read it in its entirety. If, at a later time, you wish to engage the shorter, formatted "lesson plan" version, it exists within the appendix, lesson 3c.

Today's students learn a great deal from adults who *model* appropriate behavior as well as engage the classroom instruction of it. Consequently, when dealing with adolescents, it is crucial for teachers to consider several important factors. Your pupils need to be consistently treated with honesty, compassion, patience, and respect (as well as proper discipline when necessary). A good teacher will also come to realize that his or her students need to be somewhat empowered. It is immensely beneficial if the kids feel as though they have some control over their academic and social lives on a daily basis.

Some individuals who feel totally at the mercy of others' authority stand a lesser chance of experiencing as strong a sense of motivation; of sustaining sincere commitment; and consequently, of obtaining lasting academic success. Allowing students to have a measure of control over their daily affairs strongly increases the chances of boosting their self-confidence and optimism, thus motivating them to take positive educational risks.

Addressing the self-esteem of one's students should be a goal of every teacher. When we meet our students, at some stage of adolescence, personalities are, of course, not totally developed. Rather, their personal growth is ongoing and continues to be affected by life's experiences.

As a teacher, you can provide an atmosphere that will allow self-esteem to grow and to prosper. The results among adolescents are greater self-confidence, a more satisfying educational experience, increased academic performance, fewer absences, and improved morale. Additionally, other benefits could very well be a reduction in vandalism, a rejection of substance abuse, and even abstinence from risky sexual behavior. These *reductions* are potential results of improved self-confidence and self-esteem. What better way of boosting confidence and creating a positive classroom environment than through the use of a *contract*.

At this point, your pupils can help develop the classroom's *rules and daily routine* for the coming year by constructing an agreement with the teacher. Students retain far more from their active *involvement* in an activity than from a traditional teacher-led session. The goal is to guarantee a more enjoyable, increasingly successful academic experience. The following dialogue is a suggestion:

The teacher could begin with

> As we've pointed out, one thing that may prevent a student from enthusiastically participating in a class activity could be behavior on the part of one or more classmates; or it could be something that lives within the student. Additionally, however, it could honestly be something that exists within the school environment or daily lessons. I'd like to talk about this a bit.
>
> In the past, have you taken courses that seemed unappealing, absent of any enjoyment and true academic creativity—just not what you might have been hoping for? Yeah, I know, more than likely. Have you taken courses that were just the opposite—courses that you actually enjoyed? Yes, it does make a difference in your performance.

Well, I'd like to do whatever I can to make this course one you'll remember in a positive way. In order to help us move in that direction, I'd like to develop a contract with you. As some of you may know, a contract represents two sides that come together to construct an agreement. What do you want to get out of my class this year? What are you hoping to gain?

With that, open a community meeting asking them to *brainstorm* (described here) a list of *gets*, perhaps on newsprint, a screen, or a front board, that reflect what they wish to derive from your course. (These *gets* may pertain to the curriculum or the general classroom environment and routine.)

Brainstorming

Students are encouraged to vocally state a response to a question, statement, or situation. No raising of hands is required. All responses are accepted and recorded in full view of the entire group on a board or newsprint. This encourages total involvement in a discussion and is very time efficient. They are asked to refrain from private, one-on-one conversations. (Some may be asked to repeat their suggestions if not clearly heard by the teacher or classmates.)

Withhold analyzing or questioning any of the submissions, as this may dampen enthusiasm, and some individuals might not actively engage in the activity. Responses may be evaluated at the conclusion of the activity.

Ask for clarification only when necessary, being careful not to put students in a position where they must defend their contributions. This activity works very well, allowing you to save considerable time.

- All brainstormed ideas are valid, accepted, and written down.
- Most will be reasonable. Those that are not can be dealt with later.

Some common *gets* often suggested by students: help with homework after school, individual help with such skills as writing, good grades, positive notes to parents, extra credit opportunities, homework passes, all assignments written in plain view and left there for several days, time to begin homework in class, and field trips.

Following the brainstorming, approach any suggestions that are unusable: Friday afternoons off, playing in the gym every morning, lunch daily in the classroom. In approaching the unusable suggestions, you could recognize those that would be unobtainable, or you could *ask class members* to identify any proposals that might be difficult or impossible to obtain.

- For example, point out that *Friday afternoons off* would be frowned upon by the principal, superintendent, board of education, parents, and so on—impossible. According to state law, it's also illegal. "Are there any other brainstormed items that would be difficult or impossible to obtain and, therefore, a waste of time in pursuing?" Allow students time to identify them, and ask their permission to eliminate those strongly unlikely to be accepted.
- You could suggest substituting something else. Rather than having Fridays off, perhaps use part of one class each semester or an after-school period to celebrate a holiday. Write it down.
- Additionally, your own schedule would not allow you to eat in the room on a daily basis, but would you be willing to arrange it once or twice during the course of the year?
- Making these types of concessions can display your willingness to work with the class to construct a meaningful contract.

Next, disclose a prepared list of your additional contributions—your *gives*:

- Time and energy
- Teaching to the best of my ability
- Knowledge
- Respect
- Friendship
- Patience
- Humor

Perhaps offer the *Early-Bird Special* described in chapter 4.

And finally, a last *give*, possibly similar to one of the following—go on a hike, go swimming, have a dance, have a picnic—something absolutely chosen by the teacher to get their attention while driving home the unique quality of the *contract*. As a surprise, why not drop down a sheet of newsprint hanging on the wall with the words, "Go swimming in the community pool!" and "Stop at McDonald's on the way home." They would be in disbelief—and they would love it! Needless to say, the contract makes a major influence.

Disclose a list of *nonnegotiables*. Try not to make it too long. Examples:

- No violence.
- No put-downs or bullying.
- No lying.

At this point, they may brainstorm their list of gives to get: "Please recall the definition of a *contract*. A contract is a signed piece of paper that represents an agreement constructed by two sides that come together to put a plan in action. Take a look at your list of gets. Now, what are you willing to give *me* in order to obtain them?" What are they willing to *give* so as to receive their list of *gets*?

If, in your view, certain necessary class *gives* are not suggested by students (homework on time, punctual arrival, good study habits, etc.), ask that they put themselves in your position for a moment; what would they ask for if they were teachers in charge of instruction? Or, if necessary, you could simply make a request.

Finally, review all brainstormed items.

This activity establishes a climate of cooperation within the room. It also utilizes positive peer pressure in keeping fellow students on task and conscientiously committed to success. And, of course, it's *unconventional*.

If a student, perhaps, finds difficulty in cooperating in some way, then you may initiate a *private* contract with only that individual. This approach allows room for negotiation while leaving the student's dignity intact. We need to remember how influential our behavior can be with these young people. Treating them with dignity not only generates greater potential for the development of their self-worth, but it also models appropriate behavior that can frequently sustain positive relationships within their group of peers and with the teacher.

Is it possible that several students may not be in compliance with the contract? Not likely but possible. Consequently, the teacher would then have to dissolve it, throw out the document. However, if you wait a few days, very likely one or more students may approach you asking to consider negotiating again. If they don't approach you, it would certainly be reasonable for you to eventually find a way to bring the word *contract* back into a classroom discussion.

"What if?" If one or two students don't abide by an existing contract, you could ask them, as well as the class as a whole, if they prefer that the individuals simply not participate. If there were few gives on the part of the nonparticipating pupils, then they would receive few gets. If there were no discernible grudges, then that would simply be the way it would be.[8]

Chapter Seven

The Seat of Distinction
Promoting Sensitivity, Trust, *and* Comfort

The following activity includes all lesson details used in its development. The reader is asked to initially read it in its entirety. If, at a later time, you wish to engage the shorter, formatted "lesson plan" version, it exists within the appendix, lesson 4.

The next step: Continue improving the cooperative environment.

Their behavior, at times, can be erratic, concerning, confusing, infuriating, and offensive. We know this. It doesn't mean, however, that we should sit idly by as it occurs without intervening. And most certainly, we must not ignore acts of bullying *or* self-disapproval among these young people. Increasingly, more educational professionals identify the school setting as a potential source of coercion for our students—to some extent academically but certainly socially.

Though it is a necessary and healthy practice to hold students accountable for taking on scholastic challenges, we must also keep in mind that we work with impressionable young minds that are frequently exposed to social intimidation and even physical threats emanating from their peers. These potential sources of bullying (authentic or imagined) often serve to alienate our young and cause them to withdraw from social and, subsequently, academic endeavors. Additionally, there exist more grievous consequences of social harassment within society, such as physical injury to oneself, harm to others, and even suicide.

Many of these youngsters require help in recognizing that most adolescents have similar concerns and uncertainties about peer interaction. One major uncertainty they have: How does a kid go about successfully dealing with fellow students on a daily basis? They can be made to clearly understand that there are no *winners* when insults are hurled at one another and that everyone comes out ahead when support and empathy are used within the classroom environment.

There are methods to promote a greater sensitivity to the feelings of others and thereby create more positive relationships among classmates. Likewise, pointless *self*-criticism can also lead to an unhealthy pattern of behavior, which, in the long run, may negatively affect a student's academic performance as well as physical well-being.

Many teachers believe that the school arena can actually be used as a venue within which students may take a closer look at the challenges described previously. Peer criticism, too often a major problem, can be a frequent occurrence. With the use of the following technique, this challenge can be affected. Class members can discuss a social problem, analyze it, and ultimately reduce its affect.

When the *seat of distinction* is employed, the kids themselves are directly involved in developing a solution to the *put-down* concern. With direct involvement, kids retain the inspiration motivated by the activity for a longer period of time. The following session encourages sensitivity to the feelings of others *and* reinforces the students' positive attitudes about themselves, thereby reducing the possibility of self-deprecation.

Sensitivity to feelings of peers +
reduction of self-deprecation =
less bullying, more environmental comfort,
and greater academic success

Hence, success within the realm of education is encouraged and improved.

I. The Seat of Distinction (building a level of trust and comfort among students)
   A. This activity can provide opportunities for students to engage in honest communication, encouraging peer acceptance and bonding while discouraging injuries to pride and egos through bullying or any other inappropriate behavior.
      1. The lesson encourages the opening of valuable lines of communication and promoting tolerance, understanding, and the reality that everyone possesses valuable qualities. It additionally

advocates the certainty that we experience similar needs and that our treatment of classmates strongly affects their feelings and self-esteem.
2. It provides students with opportunities to experience sincere complimentary messages from peers who would, in all probability, not have taken the time to express those positive thoughts if not involved in this activity.

B. Students will demonstrate personally and socially responsible behaviors. They will display respect for themselves and others.

    Purposes of the lesson:
1. To open positive lines of communication
2. To enhance self-esteem
3. To give class members opportunities to offer and hear sincere complimentary messages
4. To practice accepting sincere compliments without an attempt to deflect them
5. To address the ramifications of pointless criticism and bullying
6. To demonstrate our common needs
7. To reduce or eliminate self-disapproval
8. To break barriers and enhance relationships
9. To underscore the reality that every classmate possesses positive qualities

II. Procedure

A. Role-play an example of strong criticism with a student who's been made aware of the lesson's objective and has consented to taking part in the role-play. (Other students are not to be made aware of the role-play.)

    Example (with voice somewhat raised):

"Bruce, you've forgotten your homework again!
You'll never learn! You're nothing more than a failure!
Why can't you be more like Mary?"

B. Then, direct the students' attention to a SMART Board or drop a rolled sheet of newsprint that reads: "What may the result be if a person frequently hears severe criticism?"—making the class aware that it was a role-play. (Aside: "Nice going, Bruce. We had them believing it.")

C. Have the class brainstorm responses to the question. Examples: "He'll feel dumb." "She'll really begin to believe it." "He'll have little self-confidence." "She'll withdraw, not do well in school, not want to participate, want to do harm to herself." Display the printed responses in the front of the room.
D. Discuss. On newsprint, SMART Board, and the like: "What's easier to do: criticize or compliment someone?" (Obviously, criticize.)
   1. As an example, ask students to raise their hands if they can think of two or three compliments they can direct toward the school cafeteria. (Don't expect a flood of responses.) Then, following a short discussion, ask for two or three critical comments. (Which were easier to obtain?) *We can always criticize. It's easy.*
E. Discuss: "Why is it that, when we are genuinely impressed by one's behavior, we seldom communicate that impression to him or her?" (Be patient with their responses if there are more than expected.)
F. Discuss: "How do you feel when someone says something nice about you?" (Good, embarrassed, worthwhile, weird, cool.)
G. "Why is it that, when we receive compliments, we sometimes deflect the praise?"

   "I think you did a great job during the volleyball game on Saturday."

   "Well, we lost. I should have been able to serve much more effectively."

   What does this tell us about our ability to accept compliments? All one really needs to say is "Thank you." Additionally, when we deflect a compliment, the *complimentor* may feel that his or her comment has been discounted and therefore is being ignored.

   This introduction initiates several discussions on its own. Consequently, it may easily take a full period, or even longer, to complete. It is beneficial, however, if students are totally focused on the theme.
H. Instructions: The Seat of Distinction. Explain that each class member will have the opportunity to receive positive messages from classmates when sitting in *the chair*.

   Ground rules:

1. All compliments must be of a sincere and honest nature; they must deal with personal achievements or qualities, not with appearance. ("I like your sneakers.")
2. The chair occupant may not respond to messages in any way other than saying "Thank you," if so inclined. This prevents students from deflecting a compliment; they *must* accept it.

I. Appoint five students to collectively sit apart from the class, perhaps on the side of the room. These people make up the *praising panel*. Their responsibility is to share *sincere, positive* messages with the chair's occupants. The teacher should encourage members of the praising panel to call the occupant by name and maintain eye contact. This personalizes the praise and allows it to be sincerely felt more keenly by the student sitting in the chair.
    1. Demonstrate by complimenting a student while not facing him or her and then again while maintaining eye contact. Ask which time the compliment felt more meaningful. The student may elaborate.
    2. Caution members of the praising panel to begin thinking of an honest compliment as soon as they know who will be occupying the seat of distinction. In this way, youngsters will not suddenly find themselves unprepared to share a sincere word of kindness. "I can't think of anything" is certainly counterproductive.
J. Other members of the class may then follow the panel with additional positive messages.
K. At the conclusion, ask the occupant of the chair:
    1. "How was the experience?" If the student responds, "Embarrassing!" then ask, "Embarrassing good or embarrassing bad?" Ask students to clarify when necessary.
    2. Ask the occupant, "Did you hear anything that you didn't expect to hear?" (Share the response with the class or pass.) Though peers may not frequently offer positive comments to each other, they more than likely *do* have thoughts of praise for their classmates, and it's worthwhile taking the opportunity to vocally offer them. Drive this home.
    3. Finally, ask the departing seat occupant, "Who'll be the next classmate to occupy the 'seat of distinction'?"

L. After the student in the chair selects the next occupant, he or she taps a member of the praising panel out and replaces that individual as a *complimentor*.
M. Closure: When all have occupied the chair, promote a discussion held during a community meeting. Possibly refer to the purposes of the lesson (found under I.B).
   Processing this event, as described in the section on the "Milling Assassin," helps promote an even better understanding.
III. Assessment Tools and Techniques
   A. Following the experience, continue to listen for daily exchanges that reflect the main points of the lesson. With the students' permission, perhaps bring them to the class's attention. Students' intentions should be to offer comments that:
      1. demonstrate respect for themselves and others;
      2. demonstrate personally and socially responsible behaviors;
      3. acknowledge the benefits of accepting praise from peers;
      4. express the idea that deflecting compliments serves no one's best interest;
      5. acknowledge our common needs for acceptance;
      6. recognize that ways in which peers are treated may affect one's feelings, self-confidence, and academic and social success;
      7. identify the need for tolerance, understanding, and empathy;
      8. reflect the idea that, when complimentary thoughts occur, they should most often be *expressed*;
      9. accept the idea that compliments *feel good* to the complimentor as well as to the person being praised; or
      10. acknowledge that it's very easy to criticize.
   B. Prior to the community meeting, students may pair up in twos or fours and discuss the experience by applying active listening skills. Possibly assign an essay on the "Seat of Distinction."
   C. Observe the social interaction of your pupils in determining the impression made by the activity.
   D. Students may discuss behavior changes observed that they believe can be attributed to experiencing the lesson.

IV. Reflection
   A. It may be advantageous to have exposed the class earlier to any lessons addressing put-downs, tolerance, compassion, diversity, fairness, and unnecessary criticism before initiating the "Seat of Distinction." These experiences help set the stage for the activity, reduce possible intimidation, and promote a greater level of understanding and comfort with the teacher.

TESTIMONY

A group of older students who had experienced the "Seat of Distinction" years earlier were asked if they remembered the activity and if they would respond to a question based on the lesson. (On occasion, the activity was also called the "Hot Seat.")

The question, simply stated, was "What do you remember about an activity within which you participated while a sixth-grader called the 'Seat of Distinction'?"

Responses from participants (absolutely unaltered):

Kate: I enjoyed the "Hot Seat." When I was in the "Hot Seat," I felt many things, but everything I felt was good. I felt embarrassed, comforted, liked, excited, thoughtful, warm, wanted, and useful. The hot seat gives a boost of confidence. I think the hot seat is a wonderful idea.

Tammy: Thinking back to sixth grade, there are many memories. The "Hot Seat" stood out to me because it changed the way I thought of myself and other students. By sharing only positive comments with each other, the students, including myself, really began to feel better about themselves. I know that I, personally, realized that I have many great qualities that, perhaps, I was overlooking. Too many children focus on the negative qualities they "think" they have. Maybe that has to do with being at "that awkward age." The "Hot Seat" made me realize what a good person I really was on the inside.

Bobby: There are many reasons the "Hot Seat" was important to me. When I was in the "Hot Seat," I felt happy because the people were telling me my good qualities. I also felt good when I was on the praising panel because then I got to see how happy they were because I was telling them about their good qualities.

Diane's (a parent) response: As a parent of one of the students involved in experiencing the "Seat of Distinction," I recall the teacher describing this activity at a parent orientation and thinking what a wonderful lesson to help foster self-esteem and positive relationships among students.

I recall my daughter relating to us how difficult it was for her to sit in the "Hot Seat" and hear her friends say positive things and give her compliments but also how strange and wonderful she felt inside. She enjoyed sitting on the praising panel and having the opportunity to give her friends compliments where she would not be ostracized for doing so.

In a time of their development where put-downs and criticisms are seen as *cool* behavior, it was refreshing for me, as an educator and a parent, to see how the teacher was striving to encourage a positive environment and sincere compliments among these young people. I thought this was an *excellent* lesson and opportunity!

Part IV

IS THERE MORE THAT WE CAN DO?

Chapter Eight

Support Groups for Adolescents

Kids fighting. School shootings. Teenagers tragically taking their own lives. The media continues to highlight the violent responses to struggles and dilemmas existing within the lives of some of our young people. The more often kids become aware of the coverage of these responses, the more easily some may sadly come to consider them.

Too frequently, society does not teach juveniles how to resolve conflicts; they are taught, regrettably, to retaliate or to totally give up (and to some, it unfortunately appears a viable alternative to pursue). Consequently, the weight of catastrophic events such as these will hover within affected families forever.

As Americans, we quietly sit, staring at the horror on our TV screens while indulging in immense sadness and displaying expressions of misery and grief. "What can I do? I'm only one person." What can you do? What can we do? Something! We must begin constructing an approach to the problem.

Ultimately, concerned Americans must lock arms, initiating a movement toward resolving this increasing threat of violence among our nation's young. We need to become involved. The longer society waits to react, the greater the possibility that attention will drift and the less likely we'll be to begin moving strongly in a positive direction.

The tragic increase in teen violence over the last few years has greatly affected many. You will agree, something must be offered. The following concept can be very helpful. It may not be the ultimate, complete answer, but it is, you'll agree, a piece of the puzzle, an effective piece, even a proactive piece: support groups.

Though extreme violent behavior thankfully does not enter the lives of the majority of adolescents, they, too, must deal from time to time with emotional predicaments and dilemmas (confusion, discomfort, depression, anger). Consequently, support groups could offer many of our kids a measure of reassurance, comfort, and encouragement.

Our young folks are growing, changing, emerging—without a doubt, this period remains a difficult stage for some to experience. Disagreements with friends and parents, problems with schoolwork, and comments from teachers may occasionally result in unexpected, negative emotional responses.

As they begin to develop a sense of identity, adolescents more easily become confused, anxious, depressed, even angry—and cannot always identify the cause or how to deal with the emotion. Some are on the verge of entering adulthood, and this transition is more difficult today than ever before. To whom do our kids confide when in need—feeling lost, bullied, intimidated, insecure, or just overwhelmed by life?

We would prefer to say mom and dad. That would be a comfortable conclusion; kids approach their loving parents for advice, support, affection, and confidential disclosure. However, private conversations taking place between many teachers and students strongly suggest that, the majority of the time, adolescents do *not* divulge fears, confusion, emotional struggles, love interests, or other encountered difficulties to parents. They may, occasionally, reach out to a teacher or a friend, but far too frequently, the problem remains unassisted, suppressed, and consequently increases in its severity.

Studies indicate that the majority of kids *internalize* the problem. Consequently, this can lead to greater complications. How does it affect their comfort, relationships, attitude, personality, sense of trust, education, and future? Will anger set in, and could *violence* result?

One way to help our kids through these challenging times is with the development of student support groups. This is not to imply, however, that anyone and everyone in the teaching profession can nor should take on this project. You may not wish to tread into areas where you do not feel comfortable, or you may not have the support of the administration, the board of education, or even your colleagues in entering the world of private and personal student struggles. However, if this venture *can* be approached and you are interested, please read on.

This concept targets a vulnerable age group, introducing the kids to a protected setting where they may begin interacting and building trust. The sessions are organized in an effort to give the youths a forum within which to express, explore, and better understand ensuing emotions. Within the group, they easily come to realize that they are not alone in suffering misgivings and reservations. Students attending such gatherings can learn more about the world of adolescence while acquiring the skills to deal with personal concerns. The end result: the development of *greater self-assurance.*

In time, they become aware of familiar concerns existing in the lives of other group members as well as how they are perceived by their peers. Thus, they more easily gain measured confidence. With greater assurance acquired, they can develop and practice new behaviors and thus better understand how to deal with the many problems life can present during this potentially threatening period.

FACILITATOR

Now, how does a classroom teacher prepare to take on the role of a group facilitator? The truth is that there is no simple answer. To begin with, one must feel comfortable with the challenge to be undertaken and make a sincere vow to seek advice from appropriate professionals when necessary.

How would the facilitator go about developing an approach and final plan? First of all, it would be best if anyone interested in facilitating did his or her own research, possibly interviewing the professionals for advice: school psychologists, clinical psychologists, guidance counselors, the principal, and the superintendent.

Would a course in adolescent psychology be helpful? It would, more than likely, prove to be considerably useful. However, the most powerful driving force in developing a successful approach to help group members is a *desire to make things better* for them. If that is the chief motivator for your involvement, then you are truly in the right frame of mind, moving in the right direction. Of *primary* importance: sincere concern—they need someone to *listen* (and, of course, to care). OK, so, where can you begin?

Progress can be made in reading available material from appropriate texts or tapping into the abundant information accessible online. Additionally, as mentioned earlier, there is nothing wrong with reaching out to professionals within the fields of counseling and psychology to acquire methods of approaching the task.

Would any nearby professional be willing to offer you a short session or personal advice based on adolescent support group management? This manner of professional guidance should prove to be instrumental. Then again, you know these kids well. You're around them nearly two hundred days a year. You've observed them, scolded them, laughed with them, spoken one on one with them. They trust you. Aren't you a *valuable* professional? Your abilities and perceptions are valuable as well.

In preparing the young members of support groups within the school environment, honestly explain that you might not be qualified to answer *all* questions and may possibly *pass* if they inquire about subjects of which you know little. The facilitator can certainly put an answer to a member's question on hold until the next session. There would be time, therefore, to contact a qualified individual from whom to confidentially obtain pertinent information.

You are obviously *not* the psychological expert; you are the *teacher* who is giving your students an opportunity to speak, to vent, to share, to help. There is, however, a limit as to what you can provide. Additionally, it would be proper to inform members that confidentiality would be absolute on your part—unless, of course, you become aware of potential harm (physical or mental) to any individual. In that case, you would be obligated to speak out and properly *seek appropriate help* for the individual(s) involved. Referring the young people to professionals may be, at times, the only option. The specialists providing additional assistance would be *any* experts having the authority to prevent physical or mental harm to anyone.

We can assume the administration, and perhaps the board of education, would most likely have to give you their blessings before you take on the responsibility.

What Personality Traits Would Help Make a Successful Facilitator?

The facilitator would need to be proficient at:

- seeing the world through the eyes of an adolescent;
- being perceptive and able to read a kid's facial expression and body language, assessing the *slow walk, tipped head*, interpreting eye contact (or lack of it);

- anticipating certain moods or personality traits based on how students maneuver, speak (volume and intensity), and physically carry themselves;
- using emotional intelligence—being aware of one's own emotions as well as recognizing emotions in others and responding appropriately;
- having a good rapport with kids;
- having an active sense of humor;
- being considerably patient; and
- having respect for one's students.

What Can the Group Provide?

The group can provide an environment within which students may express their genuine feelings, discuss ensuing emotional issues, build self-confidence and self-esteem, deal honestly with peers, as well as gather pride and satisfaction when *being of help to other members*. Participants may more clearly see their own positive purposes in life.

- Through group sessions, participants can learn to better understand and deal with their own insecurities as they discover that most of their peers often experience similar confusion, discomfort, annoyance, and uncertainties.
- These young people can be encouraged to voice opinions, seek answers, and deal honestly with themselves and others.
- They obtain the crucial gratification of having others quietly and sincerely listen to their problems without interruption.
- The more often a member hears innermost revelations expressed by a peer, the more likely the member is to *reveal* his or her own most personal concerns.
- Students, through open dialogue, may come to better understand fellow classmates (as well as themselves).
- Within the protected setting, they are free to bounce ideas off other members whenever they feel the motivation.
- The setting also offers pupils opportunities to display their authentic empathy for other members. In helping fellow members, they more easily experience gratification, pride, and self-respect, while realizing their potential value to others.

- They may develop the realization that they each possess the capability to come to a friend's aid in offering useful coping strategies as well as sincere support.
- With time and commitment, they can easily conclude that peers in the group do care about them, and they may come to value their support.
- Here, they have the opportunity to truly be themselves, saying whatever they wish to say in whatever way they wish to say it.

Additionally, with support, they may determine a way to better avoid:

- feelings of insecurity,
- dwindling self-esteem,
- anger in solitude, and
- the danger of resorting to *violence* as a remedy for solving problems and insecurities.

Begin by identifying the kids who would likely benefit from such an experience, and approach them in a friendly, unorthodox manner, one or two at a time. Explain that you are starting a *cool, different, private, or special* group that will meet twice a week to listen to and confidentially discuss problems, struggles, and complaints that members might be experiencing. Participants would be able to trust each other. Those attending would be free to talk about any difficulty being encountered for whatever length of time necessary and explain it in whatever manner they wish.

If time runs out, they may continue during the next session. When approaching the majority of prospective members, make it a point not to sound as though you think he or she *needs* help. It is simply an offer being made to a *few* of your students—the offer of an *opportunity* that they are free to accept or refuse.

The following guidelines may be shared with group members:
You may:

- express your feelings about anything,
- get to know others in the group better,
- get to know yourself better,
- bounce ideas off the other members,

- say whatever you wish in whatever manner you wish, and
- be certain that all information would be kept confidential.

A letter of explanation needs to be sent home to the parents. The following is an example:

> Adolescents sometimes experience events during the course of the school day that trigger discomfort and difficulty. Disagreements with friends, problems with schoolwork, or even comments from teachers may result in negative emotional responses on the part of numerous students. One method of helping our kids through these difficult times is forming *support groups*.
>
> Student support groups are organized in an effort to give the youths a forum within which to express, explore, and understand common emotions. Within this setting, students can develop stronger self-confidence, learn new skills, and become more aware of the support they can acquire from their classmates. They can practice newly learned responses and better understand how to deal with some the many problems life presents. Additionally, they can gather pride and satisfaction in knowing that they have the capacity to help others.
>
> One such group is currently being formed. Only a few students will have this opportunity at a time. Your child has shown an interest in participating in the organization, which will begin following this vacation. We will meet twice a week on Tuesdays and Fridays.
>
> If you agree to allow your child to participate, please fill out the attached permission slip and send it back by Friday, February 18, or the first day of school following vacation. If you have any questions, please contact me.

The sessions might take place during a period that the students generally use to seek extra help in a particular subject, employ as a study hall, volunteer to help other students or a teacher, or attend special lessons arranged by teachers or the administration. Another option would be to possibly meet immediately following lunch if enough time is available. At times it may also be practical to arrange a session at the end of the day; transportation arrangements, of course, would need to be made.

The following evaluations offer typical responses to questions used in determining success of support group sessions. The replies were collected from members of a sixth-grade support group at the culmination of a year and are authentic:

"What, in your opinion, is the purpose of our sessions held twice a week?"
- To help people feel good about themselves.
- To let our feelings out and to seek answers to our problems.
- To be able to discuss your problems with friends and to help other people with their problems.
- To help and be helped.
- To let children deal with their feelings.
- To help people if they have problems.
- The group's purpose of meeting is so children can express feelings.

"Have our sessions been of help to you? If so, how?"
- Yes because we are all nice people.
- Definitely! It gives me an outlet for my feelings, and it lets me help others. It makes me feel good to know I can help the other kids.
- Yes because I've been able to help other people with their problems.
- Yes. I like helping people and having someone to talk to.
- Yes. I can express myself in a way I never do.
- To say what I have kept inside all this time.
- Yes because the group helped me get closer to my father.

"What did you like least about them?"
- Nothing.
- That we only had them twice a week, and *then*, they had to stop completely!!! (end of year)
- The end. And people have sad problems.
- Time!
- Not lots of time.
- I like everything.
- Nothing.

"Are there any suggestions that you could make to improve future group sessions?"
- No, not that I could think of.
- Have more of them!
- No, the sessions are good as they are.

- ?
- No.
- That we should get more people in here to tell if they have any problems.
- I have no suggestions. The group is great. I just wish we could meet for a longer period of time.

"General comments"
- I like the group very much.
- Rap on!
- I like this group, and I wish there was more time.
- Hopefully, I helped.
- It was fun. I hope for years that will follow (others) will enjoy the experience.
- It was great coming.
- My father and I are now much closer.

HOW TO BEGIN

Members need to feel welcome and comfortable before beginning to share their private concerns and feelings. This would be the first of the facilitator's objectives. Do not expect that individuals will immediately begin divulging private, personal information about themselves. It may take a bit of time. *The stage must be set.*

However, when you become better versed, so to speak, in the art of welcoming and relaxing the members of your groups, there will likely be occasions when they come ready to speak and actually do.

In addition to any preparatory strategies you may assemble through your own means, here are a few additional suggestions:

- Ease the members into the group setting in a warm and friendly manner. Then, after making sure everyone is acquainted, ask them to describe what they believe is the group's purpose.
- Clear up any misconceptions immediately.
- Stress the importance of confidentiality and respect.
- Ask everyone, "Why did you agree to join?"

- Be patient with members; it may take a bit of time before they begin divulging their problems.
- Additionally, instruct all members to also be patient rather than to interrupt their classmates; it is not a casual conversation.
- Request that the speaker let everyone know when he or she has concluded; for example, by saying "I'm done." It is not always apparent to all that the individual has completed describing the problem and is waiting for responses.
- At times, a group member may forget to announce that he or she has completed describing a concern. Therefore, after an appropriate amount of time, someone may simply ask, "Do you have more to say, Mary?"
- If you perceive, however, that the individual has concluded, then it would be appropriate for you to comment, for example, "Nicely done, Mary. If anyone wishes to respond to Mary's concerns, now would be the time." Or you could make comments, perhaps leading her in thought. Nudge her a bit in a "helpful direction." Or, if it's time to wind up, "Mary, are you comfortable with putting some of the suggestions to work for yourself?" "Perhaps think about your current experience, and let us know in our next session as to your decisions or how you've progressed."
- Remind all members to wait for an appropriate amount of time before checking with the speaker for completion.
- Once having begun, get other members involved: "What is your reaction to Mary's problem, Sam?" "Has anyone else had a similar experience?"
- Don't move in quickly *to save the day*. *Quick-fix* remedies may give the student the impression that you think he or she is "not smart enough" to figure it out alone. Toss in questions, possibly guiding the speaker in a direction to a solution. Look around, perceiving members' expressions. Then, perhaps ask one of them for a comment.
- Give group members, rather than the facilitator, the first opportunity to suggest possible directions upon which to embark.
- Don't take the floor away by stating that you totally understand the difficulty and easily propose a solution. "Same thing happened to me when I was your age. Here's what I did."

- Preach *patience* whenever possible. Repeat from time to time that they may have to put their concerns on hold for a time, maybe even until the next session.
- If tears are shed, absolutely do not say anything like, "It's OK, Jeanie, it's OK." If all were OK, then she would not be crying. Sadness and tears are part of living, just as are laughter and joy. Allow Jeanie to express her feelings openly. (And always have tissues available for Jeanie and anyone else emotionally moved by her tears.)
- Avoid making judgments: "You're taking this too seriously." "I'd just stop talking to that person if I were you." This does *not* help. Caution members to also avoid this approach.
- Do not minimize the problem: "I'm sure you'll feel differently about this in a week or so." Again, it is not the solution to the existing problem for the kid.
- As you near the end of the year, with few sessions remaining, you might have a short discussion in which you remind them how many gatherings are left. Possibly pursue the question "What will you do about any personal concerns once the group no longer meets?" "How will you deal with any problems?" "Whom will you talk to about difficulties?" And let them know how you feel about the sessions and the bonds: "I will miss seeing you and talking to you after the year ends, but I won't forget you."

At typical group sessions, members may discuss difficulties occurring between students, among family members, and amid students and teachers. On other occasions, you may hear of difficulties relating to the loss of family members or pets, misunderstandings between friends, the emotional confusion regarding parental discipline, and so much more.

Many of the concerns will be typical and expected from adolescents. Though you may be correct in assuming that some of the concerns will be discarded in a short time, they are important to the students on *that particular day*. Consequently, it is imperative for the group to focus on the concerns and offer support. Members need to feel that they can always rely on the group for support, suggestions, and encouragement.

From time to time, you may find it necessary to enlist the assistance of certain colleagues and professionals, as indicated earlier. However, suggestions offered by members of the group may frequently make very good sense to the recipients as well as to you—sometimes surprisingly so.

The support group is not the *final* answer to all adolescent difficulties. However, it does provide *an* answer, *one* piece of the puzzle. Will it turn the life of a potential bully or brooding, depressed teen around 180 degrees? Possibly. But even if not, it may get his or her attention for a period of time. And during that interval, you have the opportunity to apply a thought-out, strategic means of intervention (clinical or otherwise) that may very well motivate the individual to

- recognize the peer support available and, additionally, his or her potential;
- reconsider the value and encouragement of his or her peers; and
- most importantly, reduce or even avoid the options of anger or violence.

TESTIMONY FROM FORMER MEMBERS

The following are comments made by two former support group members. The individuals today are in their late twenties. The responses sum up what they recall from their support group experiences:

David, presently a fifth-grade *teacher*: Looking back to my sixth-grade experiences as a member of an organized support group, there are several memories that stick in my mind.

One of which is trustworthiness, both by the facilitator and the other group members. The group consisted of several students from differing backgrounds, abilities, and interests. Although I will openly admit my past hesitance to even join the group because of this and my speculation that other students had the same apprehension (because most sixth-graders would normally prefer a group to be filled solely with their best of friends), our facilitator established a safe and secure environment that made all members feel comfortable.

Right from the first meeting, we knew that whatever was spoken in the group was confidential. We knew that we had a responsibility to respect each other's thoughts and feelings. No matter everyone's background, we were at the same level here. We could communicate openly, without fear of peer judgment.

I also remember the group's sincerity. Because of the environment that was developed by the facilitator, we felt comfortable being active participants. Kids were honest and open with each other, and our mediator was always the same with us. Speakers sometimes wore their hearts on their sleeves, as did some listeners. I still recall specific accounts from sixth grade because of the emotions attached. We all resonated with each other's stories in some way, and we bonded together as the sessions continued.

Most of all, I remember the kinship. We were united by each other's personal stories and words of encouragement. I remember moments of sadness and moments of uplifting, and I always felt accepted.

Looking back at my experience from the scope of a teacher, I am even more impressed with the positivity a group such as this presents. It builds on an individual's confidence, maturity, trust, and respect. Additionally, it has a positive effect on communication and social skills, both with peers and adults. I strongly recommend a program such as this for any school.

Cory, a new dad: In 2000, when I was in the sixth grade, my English teacher approached a group of ten or so students about the formation of a "support group." We were to talk about anything, from homework to girls and boys, parents, "growing pains," or more personal things. And the best part was we were able to speak freely. Many of us didn't want to talk to our parents all the time. I struggled with problems but wouldn't talk to mine. I relied upon the group. It helped me with many difficulties.

In this day, I feel that these "support groups" would benefit many students, just to have a place to talk things out. Many kids don't get the chance to talk things out until it's too late. Too often some are resorting to physical violence to solve their problems. I believe with more groups like this, we all could help put an end to events such as Newtown or suicides. Simply listen to what the kids are trying to tell you. Everyone wants to give opinions as to what you or I should or shouldn't do but are not willing to listen to what the kids would tell them.

Chapter Nine

Multicultural Education

For years America has often been referred to as a *melting pot*. However, a more accurate, realistic term describing our country would be a *stew*. All citizens do not live a *mixture* of similar lives; they are each *different* from one another. And that's fine! This analogy is borrowed from the *A World of Difference Campaign* (its primary objective: reducing prejudice). It was sponsored by the Anti-Defamation League of B'nai B'rith under the direction of Neil and Jane Golub.

Ethnicity, religion, skin color, language, culture. These *differences* exist within our nation, with each being a chunk, a part, of America. The question is, Are the majority of our people truly becoming more accepting, understanding, tolerant, and less prejudiced? Many agree that a positive movement is underway; the country is, indeed, progressing in the right direction. A helpful strategy would be for our teachers to enhance the transition by developing the kind of programs that give our younger generation opportunities to move even closer together in learning, understanding, accepting—and celebrating—different cultural traditions.

In this way, our citizens can be encouraged *to share the diversities*. Americans can live their lives while still enjoying and occasionally taking part in each other's ethnic diversities and celebrations rather than existing in separate cultures isolated from one another. Consequently, the movement toward a society where everyone is truly understood and accepted will be more widely achieved.

Our teachers can do much to enhance multicultural acceptance while countering the existence of bigotry in our nation. Not by lecturing, however.

Sermonizing changes little in student attitudes toward different cultures. Becoming personally involved in multicultural education, on the other hand, provides our kids with experiences more easily directed toward accepting dissimilarities as well as developing the skills necessary in recognizing and rejecting prejudiced behaviors. Too many regard the unfamiliar with suspicion and aversion. Logical strategies to employ, therefore, would be to

- acquaint our kids with cultures that may appear unfamiliar to them,
- allow our young people to see evidence that ethnic groups from many parts of the world have made significant contributions to the American experience, and
- view these multicultural achievements taking place in America as evidence that we share a kinship with one another.

Each minority has the right, of course, to enjoy its heritage. Members experience greater pride, identity, and resilience when their own roots are explored and appreciated. Additionally, when a majority of our American population succeeds in comingling and sharing dialogue based on ethnicity, even more meaningful progress is achieved.

By introducing an actual *multicultural curriculum* with enlightening classroom activities, teachers can promote the idea that diversity is a strength of our nation, not a liability. This principle would help to nurture the harmony necessary for a brighter, more prosperous future for generations. Opposing arguments foster anger, disenchantment, and failure on the part of our culture.

A reduction in prejudiced thoughts and behaviors is more likely experienced by students when appropriate classroom activities are used that require them to become *personally* involved in the lesson. Teachers can approach this topic by discussing term definitions as well as reading books or other forms of literature based on such topics as

- prejudice;
- discrimination;
- stereotyping;
- scapegoating;
- apartheid;

- racism;
- tolerance;
- the Holocaust;
- the Japanese American evacuation during World War II;
- the Montgomery County bus boycott; and
- the lives of Martin Luther King and Rosa Parks, as well as a number of other related topics, themes, or associated individuals.

Students may read silently or orally, discussing the topics at length. This helps them in developing a greater understanding and appreciation for America's cultural differences, as well as an awareness of the difficulties some members of ethnic groups have had to manage.

The class, as a whole, will come to understand that we are not a homogeneous society. We are different. And these dissimilarities should be viewed as complementary. We need to reach out to one another and share our differences, celebrate them, and enjoy them.

The theme of avoiding prejudice can be pursued in reading, writing, and discussions held within class community meetings. The teacher can also include a list of spelling or vocabulary words based on the theme as well: prejudice, stereotyping, tolerance, scapegoating, bigotry, and so on. In addition to holding participants responsible for the correct spelling, they can also be quizzed on the definitions and proper manner to use the words in sentences. This tactic strongly enhances the important themes of tolerance and compassion while emphasizing the uselessness of discrimination.

Another approach: The teacher can share with the class authentic stories based on prejudice and discrimination.

Following class discussions, writing assignments could thereafter be promoted that deal with unit topics. Suggestions could then be sought for how individuals may confront the problems.

Examples:

- What would it be like if you were treated differently because of a physical characteristic over which you had absolutely no control?
- Describe an example or two of prejudiced behavior that you've witnessed at some time in your life.

Compositions could be shared and discussed with classmates, first in groups of four, and then with the entire class. Instructions follow:

1. Read your draft silently. Next, turn your paper over, and while waiting for the three other members of your quartet to finish reading their pieces, think about the behaviors you've described. How do you honestly feel about them?
2. Discuss the compositions and the difficulties suffered with your three classmates.
3. Describe something you learned about one of the issues discussed.
4. Describe something you learned about another group member.
5. What can be done about any of the problems shared by quartet members?
6. Who should begin taking steps to deal with any of the issues? (Obviously, each of them.)
7. Following the discussion, feel free to add anything more to your piece.

Perhaps a selection of videos could be viewed describing true accounts of discrimination in America, along with the difficulties experienced by citizens who, in the minds of some, were regarded as *different, unacceptable*, and *unequal*. Experiences like these can truly bring an understanding of the dilemma into the lives of your students.

Additionally, speakers can be brought in who might address a variety of topics dealing with prejudiced behavior as it affects victims *and* perpetrators. Presentations could be based on diversity, racism, physically challenged individuals, boycotts, scapegoats, stereotypes, ethnic jokes, and gay bashing.

Topics covered by the videos or speakers may then be discussed during community meetings as well used for themes in other writing assignments.

Notes

1. "Tell Me and I Forget," Northeast Regional Center for Safe and Drug-free Schools for the U.S. Department. of Education, p. 9.
2. "Second Order Change," Super Teams Limited, p. 22.
3. "Prescriptions," Super Teams Limited, p. 44.
4. "Listening Skills," ibid., p. 51.
5. "The Milling Assassin," Patricia J. Kimmerling, *Teaching Strategies for Values Clarification* (May 1, 1974), p. 58.
6. "Processing the Activity," Super Teams Limited, p. 60.
7. "Encouraging Positive Communication," ibid., p. 62.
8. "Affective Classroom Contract," ibid., p. 70.

Appendix

LESSON PLAN COMPONENTS

Lesson Title

Below is a list of seven separate lesson plan components. In some cases, however, a component or two may not be included within the lesson. Example: With some lessons, no preparatory information needs to be shared with students. Therefore, the component "Input" is not included in the lesson. The same with "Independent Practice." If the lesson has no individual classwork or homework needing to be completed, "Independent Practice" is excluded.

Objectives: Expected learner outcomes, purpose(s), goal(s) of the lesson.

Anticipatory Set: Specific activities or statements used to motivate students and to focus them on the lesson. This opening connects the students to the upcoming lesson.

Input: Information provided that is essential for the students to know before beginning the lesson. This segment also explains how the information will be communicated to them.

Instruction: Procedure and content of lesson. Presentation of concepts and lesson information.

Guided Practice: While supervised, students are led through activities that give them the opportunity to practice and apply the skills or information provided to them.

Closure: How the lesson will be "wrapped up." This is where the lesson is reviewed and the purpose is given meaning.

Independent Practice: Homework or seatwork assigned to ensure that they've mastered the skills, along with understanding the lesson's purpose and goals.

LESSON PLANS

Lesson 1: Recipe for Homework Success (Chapter 4)

Objectives

1. To allow pupils to freely discuss and even vent difficulties incurred while addressing homework assignments.
2. To encourage class members to consider *why* homework is given.
3. To engage students in an active session within which they discuss and share potentially worthwhile approaches in successfully completing homework assignments.
4. To develop a list of homework strategies for all to consider using in the future.

Anticipatory Set

1. Initiate a discussion based on homework, encouraging positive as well as negative comments. (Possibly begin by offering an earlier experience with a challenging homework assignment from your own past or from a former student's encounter.)
2. Be clear that any honest response is welcome. Responses offered by students may be written on newsprint, SMART Board, and so on by the teacher.

Instruction

1. Divide students into groups of two, directing them to focus on complaints expressed by classmates earlier in the lesson and to discuss ways of addressing the concerns in a positive fashion. (If they wish, students may take notes.)
2. After bringing the group back together in a community meeting, ask that they brainstorm solutions one concern at a time as you write them clearly on a SMART Board, newsprint, and so on.

3. Edit the brainstormed list of suggestions until the students are satisfied that the list poses strong, usable strategies for dealing with the homework concerns.
4. Display the list clearly in the classroom. At a later time, present each student with individual copies to use when faced with similar concerns.

Check for Understanding

1. Refer to the list of suggestions in the future whenever appropriate.
2. Ask the class to reflect on and share any strategies they identified as helpful in successfully completing complicated assignments.

The following is a list of those suggestions mentioned most often in my classes:

1. Don't forget to use your assignment pad, iPod, iPad, or smartphone to *keep track of assignments*.
2. Be sure that you *understand the directions* before leaving school.
3. Make good use of *study halls*.
4. *Organize your materials* in your binder and in your locker.
5. Do your work at the same time daily. *Follow a schedule*.
6. Find a quiet, comfortable *place to work*—away from the TV.
7. *Don't procrastinate*.
8. Take a *break* if you have a lot to do.
9. Put completed homework in a place where you *won't lose or forget it*.
10. Have someone in mind to contact when needing homework *advice*.

Refer to the list as necessary—or add to it.

Closure

At the conclusion of the original session, ask each class member to write down ways in which they may benefit through the use of the suggestions on the list.

Lesson 2: The Milling Assassin (Chapter 6)

This activity functions as a first step in the process of peer acceptance and bonding, encouraging a team approach to classroom challenges.

Though it may sound rather strange at first, it has practical benefits. It works. Try it.

Objectives

1. To encourage interaction, enhance trust, reduce discomfort, and energize class members.
2. To break through potentially existing barriers among students.
3. To begin a lesson, session, week, or semester in an active, unorthodox, positive manner.

Anticipatory Set

1. Introduce the two strategies that help in dealing with personal problems, discomfort, or disappointment. (The following two strategies are helpful in *setting the stage*—getting them in an appropriate frame of mind. However, with time restraints, one or both can be eliminated if necessary.)
   a. Support Network: Friends and family members available to be approached with personal concerns. "When you are experiencing any kind of difficulties, school problems, personal problems, health concerns, anything, and feel a need for support and advice, what steps can you take?" (Seek trusted friends and family.) This is essential for everyone. We all need support at times in our lives.
      - Without disclosing names of friends or family, each student is encouraged to have one or more individuals in mind during the lesson.
      - Briefly discuss examples of support experienced by teacher and class members, along with the advantages of utilizing the support.
   b. Active Sense of Humor: Humor can help *reframe* potentially depressing situations, promote the release of endorphins, and build resilience within the individual. A well-functioning sense of humor helps one see difficult situations in a different, more realistic light.
      - Offer amusing occurrences from your life that helped you deal with challenging times. Ask for humorous examples from the class. Brief discussion.
      - Then, taking advantage of their amused frames of mind, move immediately from the existing humorous environment into the following activity.

Instruction

1. Introduce the "Milling Assassin," explaining rules and procedure beforehand.
2. Move around the outside of a circle of students standing with their eyes closed and hands open behind them.
3. Pull on the index finger of each, except for the student you've secretly chosen to portray the "Milling Assassin." Instead, touch the middle of the palm.
4. Announce: "Go ahead and mill." Students wander about silently, shaking hands (and smiling like crazy—they can't help it).
5. When *the assassin* feels he or she can get away with it, while shaking hands, the index finger is extended to touch the wrist area of the unsuspecting classmate.
6. After receiving the *death tap*, the victim silently counts to ten, then falls to the floor, making any appropriate vocal noises he or she wishes. No one else may speak. Counting to ten allows the "assassin" to move away from the victim and not be easily identified.
7. If a student feels he or she knows who the assassin is, then he or she may raise a hand and ask the facilitator to stop the action. The facilitator then asks the class for a second individual to raise a hand in order to "back up" the guess to be made by the first individual. (You need two participants involved in order to officially offer a guess to identify the assassin.) After someone volunteers to *back up* the first student, he or she is then given the opportunity to identify the assassin. If the individuals are correct, then the assassin has been successfully identified, and the first session concludes. If the individuals are incorrect, both also *die* and fall to the floor. Continue milling.

Closure

Through *processing* the activity:

This offers a *look back*, a manner of reviewing an activity in such a way that the participants better understand its purpose. They may also examine what they were thinking, feeling, and doing during the flow. They may then more easily perceive the benefits of engaging the lesson and what can be learned from it (about each other and about working together).

Processing could include the use of such helpful questions as:

- Why do you think I introduced the lesson?
- What did you learn about yourself, classmates, teacher, school?
- What surprised you?
- What would you change in the activity to make the lesson more interesting?
- How are you feeling about what we just did?

Are they in a lighter mood? Might they be viewing classmates a bit differently? Have connections and relationships among them been improved?

The processing component may include the teacher simply feeding back to the kids what he or she had observed—speed with which work was done, conversations engaged, who got out of the chair first, who approached a classmate quickly or slowly, first or last, who smiled, and so on—in order to allow the class an opportunity to review the activity and understand participants' different interpretations of the task.

Example:

> I observed several rise from their chairs rather quickly and begin forming a circle when told to do so. The majority of the class, however, rose more slowly, heads turning to look around the room, and did not seem to be in a hurry. Once the exercise was underway, there were smiles and laughter. This appears rather normal for a group this size. I've seen the same reaction with high school seniors, teachers, and even parents when engaged in this activity. Now, I could be wrong, but some seemed, well, a bit reluctant at first to get moving but then eventually joined in. I loved every moment!

The practice of *processing* helps everyone understand how the class is doing and validates the reality that some class members have different perceptions and reactions to the task. They may come to recognize that their classmates view the lesson a bit differently, and it may even give them a new perspective on the activity as well as on their peers.

Additionally, some may respond to future classroom encounters with greater enthusiasm and optimism and less hesitancy.

Repeat the activity if there is time and interest.

Lesson 3: Encouraging Positive Communication

A series of three lessons, with the fully detailed format appearing in chapter 6.

Lesson 3a: Introduction to Successful Listening

Objectives

1. To describe and practice useful listening skills that help students to successfully engage in total comprehension during conversations.
2. To understand and avoid barriers to communication.

Anticipatory Set

As an introduction, you could offer the following questions to the class in considering the frequent problems many experience in communicating with others:

- How well do members of our society listen to each other?
- How do you know when an individual is listening to you? (One can judge by behavior, body language, facial expressions, etc.)
- How do you know when an individual is *not* listening to you?
- How does one *feel* when a person is listening?
- How does one feel when a person is *not* listening?
- Why is it sometimes difficult to listen?
- What does it mean to *actively* listen? (Any responses similar to the behaviors listed under "Instruction" would be encouraging.)
- Why is listening important?

Instruction

Discuss the following basic listening requirements:

- Make solid eye contact, and lean into the conversation, nodding when motivated to do so.

- Try to be accepting, even if you initially disagree.
- As the individual is speaking, use *cultural fillers* ("Is that right?" "I understand." "Really!" "Tell me more." "Uh-huh."). In this way, the speaker knows you are listening intently.
- Encourage more communication: "Tell me more." "Would you like to talk about it?" "How did you feel about that?" "Then, what happened?"

Stop listening!

As a method of underscoring the importance of listening, ask a student to speak to you about an important topic. Encourage the individual to choose a topic that is recent, significant, and known to everyone in the room.

When the discourse begins, role-play the *nonlistener*, the individual who makes minimal efforts, sounds, and gestures in persuading the speaker to believe that he or she is listening. When the speaker begins engaging the topic, behave in the following manner: eyes move quickly from side to side; head turns; glance at your wristwatch or the wall clock; continually nod much too quickly; shuffle papers on your desk; repeat, "Yep, yep"; and make little if any real eye contact.

Following the verbal attempt, ask the speaker how he or she feels about your reaction. Responses are usually something like "Left out," "Not important," "Unsuccessful," "Like you didn't care about me or what I had to say."

Then ask the individual to engage in delivering the message again. This time hold still, lean forward, maintain eye contact, nod from time to time, and use verbal cultural fillers ("I see!" "Really!" "Hard to believe!" "No kidding!" "Go on."), as well as facial responses. Once again, ask how the speaker feels. I'm sure you can easily anticipate the dissimilar reaction. Listening is something that we all need to focus on.

It is now time to introduce these effective skills and barriers:

- Reflective Listening: Feed back to the speaker words that disclose how you perceive him or her. We must listen to the feelings behind the speaker's words. Sometimes, the *listener* ends up informing the *speaker* how he or she feels. "Sounds like he made you pretty angry." "You seem really sad." "You sound anxious about this concern." "I'll

bet that's very frustrating to you." "You really get angry when he says that, don't you?"
- Paraphrasing: Let the speaker know that you've heard him or her by repeating the message in your own words. "So, you're feeling quite lonely right now because she told you she would call to plan the shopping trip and never called."
- Summarize: Highlight the main points. "Here's what I hear you saying." "If I understand you correctly, you're saying that . . ." *Condense it.*

Barriers to communication may occur when the listener is responding to the *facts* rather than to the speaker's *feelings*.

- Do not offer quick solutions: *Quick-fix* remedies may give the speaker the impression that you think he or she is not smart enough to figure it out alone.
- Avoid making judgments: "You're taking this too seriously." "I'd just stop talking to her if I were you." This does *not* help.
- Do not minimize the problem: "I'm sure you'll feel differently about this in a week or so." Again, it is not the solution to the existing problem for the speaker.
- Don't *take the floor away* from the speaker by interjecting your experience concerning a similar problem: "The same thing happened to me; here's what I did."

The speaker is looking for someone primarily to listen to him or her; *listen* is the key word.

Guided Practice

Following the coverage of these skills, instruct the class to develop a two- or three-minute message to verbally share with a classmate. The message could be based on almost anything—opinions, events, sports, future plans in life. Then, explain the strategies listed on the next page (listener and speaker responsibilities) while demonstrating how to engage them. Students should, of course, be given sufficient time to study the task in preparation.

Listener

Focusing	Attending	Reaction
-Finds a purpose for listening	-Decides whether message is organized	-Asks for further clarification
-Is prepared to deal with major distractions	-Tries to anticipate speaker's point(s) -Accepts or rejects them	-Feeds back major points
-Is ready and willing to be attentive	-Asks for clarification	-Voices concerns constructively
-Attempts to be open-minded	-Evaluates -Remains sensitive to nonverbal messages	

Speaker

Focusing	Attending	Reaction
-Prepares message with a purpose	-Presents message in a clear and organized manner	-Accepts and responds questions
-Decides what to say and how to say it	-Speaks clearly with appropriate volume and speed	-Is sensitive to listener's reaction
-Feels free to use nonverbal communication	-Is open to constructive criticism	

Figure A.1

Divide students into groups of two, one being the speaker and one being the listener. Following three- to five-minute engagements, instruct each of the two to feed back to the other thoughts and feelings concerning the exchange. What transpired? How did it succeed? Following that, reverse the roles. Another approach would be to have a duo go through the activity in the center of the room. Then, review the experience using comments from the entire class.

Lesson 3b: The Next Step: What Stops Some Students from Becoming Enthusiastically Engaged in a Class Activity?

Objective

To stimulate students' active involvement in daily lessons.

Anticipatory Set

Briefly discuss the connection between poor or mediocre involvement in daily lessons and inadequate achievement in school. How might this evolve into ultimate long-term effects?

Input

Begin a discussion centered on the connection between success within the school environment and success in life. Briefly describe the potentially everlasting results of poor grades and the difficulty in furthering one's education and acquiring a quality job. Underscore the difference in paychecks between possessing an unsatisfactory job and having well-established, respectable employment. Stress the need to do whatever necessary in developing one's potential regardless of environmental circumstances.

Consider offering something like the following:

> How important is college? Information from the federal government suggests a college degree is worth the time, work, and money invested. The vast majority of people with a college degree earn nearly twice the income

of people with only a high school degree. Additionally, college graduates are more inclined to avoid layoffs and to be employed long term. At the same time, we must clearly state that *every* student may *not* need to acquire a college degree. Valuable skills enable many to earn excellent wages while also allowing them to truly enjoy their occupations. These people must, however, sincerely work at learning their trades so as to be successful. And usually the learning begins in school.

Instruction

Introduce and pursue the following topics:

A. What is it about *others* that stops me from becoming enthusiastically engaged in a class activity?
   - Individual responses on paper. Grammar and spelling do *not* apply.
   - Discussion with a partner. Share, discuss, and make suggestions.
   - Discussion in groups of four. Share, discuss, and make suggestions.
   - Class discussion.
   - Instruct participants to silently write *prescriptions*. (This technique is introduced in chapter 4. Suggestions are made by classmates to help deal with particular concerns and then shared with the student experiencing the difficulty or with the entire class.)
   - The teacher or student reads the responses. Further discussions are at the discretion of the teacher and class. Suggestion: Walk the room during the earlier part of the lesson, observing examples of the students' use of the listening skills.

   Rationale to lesson. It gives students an opportunity to:
   - See evidence of others' frustration. (I'm not the only one.)
   - Relieve some of their frustration through discussions and venting.
   - Discover solutions to their problems.
   - See evidence of the teacher's fairness, patience, understanding, and respect.

Then:

B. What is it about *me* that stops me from becoming enthusiastically engaged in a class activity? Emphasize the importance of honesty.

Follow same process: Individual responses, discussion with partner, groups of four, class discussion, prescriptions.

Closure

Discuss responses.

Lesson 3c: Developing the Classroom Contract

Objectives

1. To empower students by having them take part in developing academic and social procedures as well as daily routines for the class.
2. To improve their motivational ambitions.
3. To create an atmosphere that will allow self-esteem and respect for peers to grow.
4. To enhance their educational experiences.
5. To help them in accepting responsibility for making significant decisions.
6. To help them develop a greater appreciation for academic challenges.

Anticipatory Set

Good teachers realize that students need to be empowered. Allowing students to have a measure of control over their daily classroom affairs strongly increases the chances of greater student participation, boosting their self-confidence and optimism and thus motivating them to take positive educational risks.

We can provide an atmosphere that will allow:

- self-esteem to grow and prosper,
- greater self-confidence,

- a more satisfying educational experience,
- increased academic performance,
- fewer absences, and
- increased morale.

This allows them to take part in developing classroom procedures that benefit everyone.

What better way of boosting confidence and helping to create a positive classroom environment than through the use of a contract, whereby the kids, along with the teacher, participate in creating academic and social guidelines along with procedures for all to abide by in the coming year. Students retain far more from their active *involvement* in classroom activities than from traditional teacher-led sessions.

Reflect on lesson 3b (The Next Step: What Stops Some Students from Becoming Enthusiastically Engaged in a Class Activity?) by beginning with something like "As we've pointed out, one thing that may prevent a student from enthusiastically participating in a class could be one or more of the other students, or it could be something that lives within the student. Additionally, however, to be totally honest with you, it could be something that exists within the school environment or daily lessons, as well. I'd like to talk about this for a while."

Input

Example:

> In the past, have you taken courses that seemed unappealing, absent of any enjoyment and true academic creativity, or are just not what you might have been hoping for? Yeah, I know, more than likely. Have you taken courses that were just the opposite, courses that you looked forward to beginning, that brimmed with interest and excitement, lessons that you actually enjoyed? Yes, it does make a difference.
>
> Well, I'd like to do whatever I can to make this course one you'll remember in a positive way. In order to help us move in that direction, I'd like to develop a contract with you.
>
> As many of you may know, a contract represents two sides that come together to construct an agreement. What do you want to get out of my class this year? What are you hoping to gain? The answers to this question would be your side of the agreement.

Instruction

With that, ask them to brainstorm aloud a list of *gets* on newsprint, a screen, or a board at the front of the room that reflects the type of class guidelines, routines, and achievements they wish to derive in taking your course. (These *gets* may pertain to the curriculum or the general classroom environment and routine.)

Brainstorming (Time-Efficient Technique)

Students freely offer vocal suggestions with no raising of hands. Each proposal is recorded in full view of the entire class. This encourages total involvement in a discussion. Do not pause to evaluate a particular submission as to its plausibility; ideas may be analyzed at the conclusion of the activity.

Ask for clarification only when absolutely necessary, being careful not to put the student in a position where he or she feels that the contribution must be defended.

All suggestions are valid and written down.

Some common *gets* suggested by students include:

- help with homework after school,
- individual help with mastering the subject matter,
- good grades,
- positive notes to parents,
- extra credit opportunities,
- homework passes,
- reading novels that students select,
- spending time reading silently in class,
- field trips, and
- all assignments written in clear view and left there for several days.

Following the brainstorming, approach any suggestions that are unusable in a nonthreatening manner (e.g., Fridays off, playing in the gym every morning, eating lunch in your room). In approaching the unusable suggestions, you could do the following:

- Point out that *Fridays off* would be frowned upon by the principal, superintendent, board of education, parents, and so on. According to

state law, it's also illegal. "Are there any other brainstormed items that would be impossible to obtain and, therefore, a waste of our time in pursuing?"
- You could suggest substituting something else. Rather than having Fridays off, perhaps use part of one class each semester to celebrate a holiday.
- Additionally, your own schedule would not allow you to eat in the room on a daily basis, but would you be willing to do it once or twice during the course of the year if it was possible to arrange? Making these types of concessions can display your willingness to work with the class and construct a meaningful contract.

Next, disclose a prepared list of your additional contributions (your *gives*):

- Time and energy
- Knowledge
- Respect
- Patience
- Humor

Other contributions on the teacher's part could certainly inspire enthusiasm:

- A trip to a community swimming pool taking place during an evening, with swimming from 6:00 until 8:00. Parents could provide transportation with three to four kids per car. The trip could conclude with a visit to McDonald's following the swim. (Expect incredible expressions.)
- Early-Bird Special: A useful strategy in persuading students to be time conscious: On days when planning to give a pop quiz, place a bonus question, along with its answer, on the board right beneath a map or large sheet of paper that can be rolled up or down. At precisely thirty seconds before the bell begins the period, pull the map or sheet of paper down to conceal the bonus question. Anyone arriving after that time misses the opportunity to obtain the bonus points. This encourages students to get to class as early as possible on a regular basis, especially because they do not know in advance when there would be a pop quiz.

Disclose another list—the *nonnegotiables* (try not to make it too long):

- No violence.
- No put-downs or bullying.
- No lying, etc.

At this point, they brainstorm their list of *gives to get*. What are they willing to *give* so as to receive their list of *gets*? If, in your view, certain necessary class *gives* are not suggested (homework on time, punctual arrival, attentive during class, etc.), ask that they put themselves in your position for a moment; what would they ask for if they were a teacher in charge of instruction? Or, if necessary, simply make a request.

Closure

Finally, review all brainstormed items, and discuss the contract.

This activity establishes a climate of cooperation within the room. It also utilizes positive peer pressure in keeping fellow students on task and conscientiously committed to success. (And, of course, it's unconventional.)

If the teacher faces a situation where a student is, perhaps, uncooperative in some way, then one may initiate a private contract with only that individual. This approach allows room for negotiation while leaving the student's dignity intact.

Treating uncooperative students with dignity not only generates greater potential for the development of their self-worth; it also obtains their attention in a positive manner while modeling appropriate behavior that can frequently help sustain positive relationships within their group of peers and with the teacher.

Lesson 4: The Seat of Distinction (Chapter 7)

This activity can provide opportunities for students to engage in honest communication, reduce or eliminate self-disapproval, encourage peer acceptance and bonding, and discourage injury to pride and egos through bullying or any other inappropriate behavior.

Objectives

1. To open positive lines of communication.
2. To enhance self-esteem.
3. To give class members opportunities to hear sincere, complimentary messages.
4. To practice accepting compliments without attempting to deflect them.
5. To address the ramifications of pointless criticism and bullying.
6. To demonstrate our common needs.
7. To reduce or eliminate self-disapproval.
8. To break barriers and enhance relationships.
9. To underscore the reality that every classmate possesses positive qualities.

Anticipatory Set

Role-play an example of strong criticism with a student who's been made aware of the lesson's objective and has consented to taking part in the role-play (discussed with the student earlier; the remainder of the students should be unaware that it is simply an act).

Example: With a somewhat raised voice: "Bruce, you've forgotten your homework again! You're nothing more than a failure! Why can't you be more like Mary?"

After a brief moment, make the class aware that it is a role-play.

Perhaps reveal its purpose by dropping a rolled sheet of newsprint or exposing a question written on a SMART Board: *"What may the result be if a person frequently hears severe criticism?"* Perhaps, address Bruce in a manner similar to the following: "We really had them believing it, huh, Bruce? You were great. Thank you."

Have the class brainstorm responses to the question. Examples: "He'll feel dumb." "She'll really begin to believe it." "He'll have little self-confidence." "She'll withdraw, not do well in school, not want to participate, want to do harm to himself."

Input

Discuss the following questions thoroughly, giving appropriate examples:

1. What's easier to do, criticize or compliment someone? (Obviously, criticize.)
2. Why is it that, when we are genuinely impressed by one's behavior, we seldom communicate that impression to him or her?
3. How do you feel when someone says something nice about you?
4. Why is it that, when we receive compliments, we sometimes deflect the praise?

Instruction

The Seat of Distinction: Explain that each class member will have the opportunity to receive positive messages from classmates when sitting in *the chair*.

Ground rules:

1. All compliments must be of a sincere and honest nature; they must deal with personal achievements or qualities, not with appearance ("I like your sneakers").
2. The chair occupant may not respond to messages in any way other than saying "Thank you." (If they are not inclined to say "Thank you," then they should remain silent. This prevents students from deflecting a compliment; they *must* accept it.)
3. Appoint five students to collectively sit apart from the class (on the side of the room, perhaps). These people make up the "praising panel." Their responsibility is to express *sincere*, *positive* messages to the chair's occupants. The teacher should encourage members of the praising panel to call the occupant by name and maintain eye contact. This personalizes the praise and allows it to be sincerely "felt" more keenly by the student sitting in the chair.

Caution members of the praising panel to begin thinking of an honest compliment as soon as they know who will be occupying the "Seat of Distinction." In this way, youngsters do not suddenly find themselves unprepared to share a sincere word of kindness. "I can't think of anything" is certainly counterproductive.

1. Eye contact is extremely important. Demonstrate by complimenting a student while not facing him or her and then again while maintaining eye contact. Ask which time the compliment felt more meaningful.
2. Other members of the class may then follow the panel with additional positive messages directed to the chair's occupant.
3. At the conclusion, ask the occupant of the chair:
   a. "How was the experience?" If the student responds, "Embarrassing!" then ask, "Embarrassing good or embarrassing bad?" (Ask students to clarify when necessary.)
   b. Ask the occupant, "Did you hear anything that you didn't expect to hear?" Share it or pass. Though peers may not frequently exchange positive comments with each other, they more than likely *do* have complimentary thoughts of their classmates, and it's worthwhile taking the opportunity to vocally offer them. Drive this home.
   c. Finally, ask the departing seat occupant, "Who'll be the next classmate to occupy the 'Seat of Distinction'?"

After the student in the chair selects the next occupant, he or she taps a member of the praising panel out and replaces that individual as a "complimentor."

Closure

When all have occupied the chair, promote a discussion based on the lesson's objectives 1 through 9.

- Following the experience, continue to listen for daily exchanges that reflect the main points of the lesson.
  a. Students' intentions should be to offer comments that
     - demonstrate respect for themselves and others;
     - demonstrate personally and socially responsible behaviors;
     - acknowledge the benefits of accepting praise from peers;
     - express the idea that deflecting compliments serves no one's best interest;
     - acknowledge our common needs for social acceptance;
     - recognize that treatment affects one's feelings, self-confidence, and academic and social success;
     - identify the need for tolerance, understanding, and empathy;

- reflect the idea that when complimentary thoughts occur, they should most often be expressed;
- accept the idea that compliments "feel good" to the complimentor as well as the person being praised; and
- acknowledge that it's very easy to criticize.

b. Consider assigning an essay on the "Seat of Distinction."
c. Students may pair up in groups of two and discuss the experience by applying active listening skills.
d. Observe the social interaction of your pupils to determine the impression made by the activity.
e. Students may discuss behavior changes observed daily that they believe can be attributed to experiencing the lesson.

Student
(unspoken words)
Victor Sgambato

My grades could be higher; I admit it.
But that doesn't mean I don't appreciate your concern.
When you're near me, I may feel a little nervous.
But that doesn't mean I don't want you to come closer.

I know I don't smile when you approach,
But please don't stop smiling at *me*.
I may not respond to your greetings, but your
Words of encouragement have become part of my life.

When you pause at my desk, your hand rests on my shoulder.
Though I don't know how to return
Your offer of warmth and friendship,
Please don't allow that to diminish your comforting support.

You're older, and your clothes are neater than mine,
But, you make me feel, I don't know,
Like—like you're my *friend*.

I'm always happy to be here—in your classroom.
In fact, at the end of the day, I don't want to leave (don't tell Mom).
When the year ends, and I don't see you every day,
I know I'm not going to like that—I don't want it to end.

About the Author

Vic Sgambato has thirty-five years of experience teaching English, writing, and health. In addition to publishing articles on education, history, and health and wellness, he's assisted in developing a curriculum resource guide to support the new learning standards in health education for the New York State Department of Education. Sgambato also developed curricula for the Fort Plain Central School District in the areas of English, health, and AIDS education.

Additionally, he is

- Fort Plain's June 1997 Teacher of the Year,
- recipient of the 1998 New York State English Council Educators of Excellence Award,
- 1992 New York State Teacher of the Year nominee,
- nominated and included in Who's Who among America's Teachers three times, and
- former trainer for the A World of Difference Campaign directed by Neal and Jane Golub.

Now retired from education, Sgambato lives with his wife in Fort Plain, New York. They have four grown children, seven grandchildren, and one spoiled chocolate lab.